Studying God

LEARNING CHURCH

Studying God: Doing Theology

Jeff Astley

scm press

© Jeff Astley 2014

Published in 2014 by SCM Press
Editorial office
3rd Floor
Invicta House
108–114 Golden Lane
London
EC1Y 0TG

SCM Press is an imprint of Hymns Ancient & Modern Ltd
(a registered charity)
13A Hellesdon Park Road
Norwich NR6 5DR, UK

www.scmpress.co.uk

Scripture quotations are from the New Revised Standard Version of the
Bible, Anglicized Edition, copyright © 1989, 1995 by the Division of
Christian Education of the National Council of the Churches of Christ in
the USA. Used by permission. All rights reserved.

British Library Cataloguing in Publication data

A catalogue record for this book is available
from the British Library

978 0 334 04414 7

Typeset by Regent Typesetting
Printed and bound by
CPI Group (UK) Ltd, Croydon

Contents

Preface

This volume in the *Learning Church Series* is for readers who are embarking for the first time on the study of Christian theology or doctrine, either as independent learners or as part of a programme of study reflecting on Christian discipleship and/or ministry.

I hope the book begins where people are in their journey of theological learning, and that it will help them make good progress across the very varied terrain of Christian thinking and believing. I believe that they can succeed in this without losing either their bearings or the insights and commitment that impelled them to take on the journey in the first place. We can travel quite a long way from home in our explorations while retaining our respect, and indeed affection, for the wisdom that we first learned there.

I do not expect readers of *Studying God: Doing Theology* to become professional academic theologians, but to develop as thinking Christians. As such, they need to be able – and to want – to listen, respond to and *use* academic theology. This is in order to help them: to help clarify and develop both how they think about God for themselves and how they can best articulate their own faith when communicating with others.

The first draft of this book was written while I was Director of the North of England Institute for Christian Education (NEICE), an ecumenical charity that devoted itself to researching and support-ing Christian learning in all its aspects from 1981 to 2013. I am grateful to the many students and adult learners I came to know through my work there, as well as in other contexts and institutions, and from whom I have learned a great deal about what it means – personally as well as intellectually – to study theology. I should like to dedicate the book to Evelyn Jackson, Administrative Secretary of NEICE for 17 years, whose skill and patience have been invaluable in preparing many works for publication, including this one.

Jeff Astley
April 2014

1

Beginning Where We Are?
You and Your Theology

'We must begin where people are' has become something of a cliché, especially in some church circles. But when we are faced with the challenge of speaking to, teaching or caring for someone – anyone – there is nowhere else to begin. All education and all pastoral care must place the other person, the one who is being taught or cared for, at the centre. In such situations it really is true that 'this is not about me, it's about you'.

You are the focus of this book and of this whole *Learning Church Series*. This is not so much a boast or even an aim, as an inevitable fact. For the reader or viewer is always the most significant person in the room when he or she reads a book or watches TV on their own; and the students or audience members are the key people in the classroom, arena, concert hall, cinema or theatre, even when they are listening to a speaker, musician, singer or actor 'live'. This is because if the readers, listeners and viewers do not 'get it', it is not got: the communication and relationship fails for them. And the same goes for caring; unless *you* are helped, 'my caring' has come to nothing.

So who are you, 'where have you come from' and (most importantly) where do you think you are going, as you read this text? Unfortunately, I cannot tailor my words specifically to you because I know nothing about you – not even your age or sex, let alone your concerns, hopes, abilities, relationships, personality or faith. But I do know this: you are *already* a theologian.

TO DO

Without discussing the question with anyone else, or looking up any other sources for help, please jot down what you understand by the word 'theologian'. What do you imagine his/her main activities to be?

Listening out for theology

Inevitably, 'the act of defining theology is part of the process of doing theology' (Franke, 2005, p. 44) – as we shall see!

The word 'theology', which is from the Greek words for 'God' and 'discourse' (or 'study'), was originally applied very widely in the Church. It described anyone who reflected on and spoke about their faith. It was many centuries before this word became restricted to the sophisticated God-talk of scholars. Today, however, it is most often used to describe university courses and departments that promote the academic study of Christianity through a variety of subject areas and using a variety of intellectual skills (see Chapter 6) and that usually cater for Christians and non-Christians alike (see Chapter 3). Part of that academic study includes studying the theology of great Christian thinkers of the past, as well as evaluating and developing current theological ideas and arguments. This is the realm of *academic theology*.

You may be such a person yourself; but it is far more likely that you have done little or no academic study of Christianity and its beliefs. Yet if you ever think about God seriously, if you ever reflect on what the Bible, hymns and other people say about God, then you are a theologian in the original sense of that word. I would call you an ordinary theologian: not intending by this adjective any slight, but recognizing that this is the 'normal', 'common', 'everyday' form of Christian theology. It is 'not unusual' or out of the way; as academic theology often is. As one (academic) theologian puts it: 'To be a good theologian is to be a Christian who thinks.' 'All

Christians already are theologians' if they take responsibility for their beliefs and if those beliefs affect their Christian lives; if they truly are 'reflective believers' (Cobb, 1993, pp. 7, 17–18, 136). This is the *broader* idea of a theologian, as a 'thinking Christian' (cf. Inbody, 2005, pp. 10–11).

This *ordinary theology* tends to use anecdotes and insights from our ordinary experience and reflections about God, mixed with wise sayings and aphorisms that we have heard from others. It is inclined to speak of God largely in metaphor and parable, in the same way that much of the theology does that we hear in Scripture and hymns. Academic theology, in particular in the area of 'doctrine' (that is, Christian teachings), develops these personal, experiential stories and other figures of speech into impersonal concepts, pruning away at the riotous natural language of the religious woodland until it is transformed into the smoother contours of shrubs in a formal theological garden. It also seeks, by using reasoned arguments, to connect these elements together 'systematically' into one pattern, so that people can more easily move from one part to another (from beliefs about Jesus to beliefs about God, for instance), instead of getting tangled up in the rather wild and disorderly, ordinary theological thicket, unable to find a route through.

All this makes academic theology seem rather superior. But I would argue that, while such systematic, careful and critical thinking about God can be very helpful, it must always relate back to the ordinary theology that lies in the heart of everyday believers and thus at the heart of the Christian Church.

In fact, ordinary theology has a religious or, better, a *spiritual* priority. It is our first theology, which arises directly from our faith, our experience and our relationship with God in worship and prayer: which themselves chiefly originate in our responses both to the gospel story and its challenges and to the reactions to these things of other Christians. Academic theology can help ordinary theology out by clarifying and critiquing it; but it can never wholly replace it. And the same may be said about much of the *ecclesiastical theology* that comes from the reflections and decisions of the Church's synods, councils and teachers down the ages – the theology of confessions, creeds and dogmas (that is, officially defined doctrines). This, like academic theology, often uses carefully honed concepts, arguments and explanations; although it may keep closer to the familiar analogies, metaphors and insights that ultimately derive from biblical texts and religious devotion and thus to the reflections of the ordinary theologian.

So, theology may be heard in different voices and forms, and in different places, while sharing much in common. But we must accept that:

> The [academic] theologian gets no new revelation and has no special organ for knowledge. He is debtor to what we, in one sense, have already – the Scriptures and the lives and thoughts of the faithful ... This puts theology within the grasp of ... someone you know down the street who shames you with his or her grasp ... Theology is often done by the unlikely. (Holmer, 1978, p. 21)

TO DO

Dig out and examine some material written by academic theologians. If you do not have access to any appropriate theological books, look on the web.

How does this material differ from the way 'ordinary' Christians talk about their faith?

Theology in conversation

It is certainly possible to develop your own ordinary theology so that it makes more sense (to you and, possibly, to others), and works better as an expression of your faith, while having little to do with academic or even ecclesiastical theology. Many people operate at this level. I assume, however, that you are reading this book and others in this series because you want to press your theology a little further and to open it up to the influence, ideas and arguments of academic theologians and the Church's teachings. (Or, perhaps, because other people have told you that you *should* engage in this task.)

I suggest that the best way of understanding that process is to see it as a sort of conversation between the reflections of your ordinary theology, on the one hand, and the voices of academic (and ecclesiastical) theology, on the other (see Chapter 3). Each of the partners in this conversation has something to say, something to contribute on their own account. But each must pay attention to the other – each must 'listen up' – and each must be willing to respond and change. You can't guarantee that your voice will change academic theology; although I have argued that in principle it sometimes should (see Astley, 2002, pp. 148–62). But you *can* make sure that you play your part in actively engaging your ordinary theology in response to what you hear from 'the academy'. As you 'take something from' this conversation, you will become engaged in further, deeper theological *learning* as your ordinary theology changes.

But, I repeat, it is not your task here to become a professional, academic theologian. Your role is to listen to, think about, respond to and *use* academic theology in order to help clarify and develop how you think about God and how you articulate the other aspects of your own faith; and how you give 'an account of the hope that is in you' (1 Peter 3.15).

Further reading

Cobb Jr, J. B., 1993, *Becoming a Thinking Christian*, Nashville, TN: Abingdon Press.

Grenz, S. J. and Olson, R. E., 1996, *Who Needs Theology? An Invitation to the Study of God*, Downers Grove, IL and Leicester: InterVarsity Press.

Inbody, T., 2005, *The Faith of the Christian Church: An Introduction to Theology*, Grand Rapids, MI: Eerdmans, Ch. 1.

West, M., Noble, G. and Todd, A., 1999, *Living Theology*, London: Darton, Longman & Todd.

Wilson, J. R., 2005, *A Primer for Christian Doctrine*, Grand Rapids, MI: Eerdmans, Ch. 1.

2

The Variety of Theology:
Its Form, Audience and Source

Doing theology in style

It will be helpful if we begin this chapter by listening in more depth
to the variety of theological reflections as they are expressed in
ordinary as well as academic theology and by attempting to discern
something of the form they take.

Ordinary theology is defined in terms of the theology embraced
by people with little or no theological education. This, if you like,
is its *location*. How might we portray the type of theology we find
here? Unlike academic theology, it tends to be marked by an absence
of technical terms and complex arguments. And its language is
more everyday, more personal and often more passionate. In these
respects, *academic* theologians can also employ ordinary theology,
by using this type of God-talk; as can – and should – theologically
educated clergy (chiefly, perhaps, in their sermons). This is possible,
because so much theology begins as ordinary theology, historically
and individually. The academic theology of the few builds on and
develops this broader foundation; and inside most academic theologians there is an ordinary theologian who first learned a different
style of God-talk that still underlies – and can give personal depth
and power to – her or his academic theology.

We may argue, then, that ordinary theology is the origin and
source, and the foundation and underpinning of much academic
God-talk; and it often functions as its life force and motivating energy.
Neither the academy's arguments or the Church's pronouncements

can afford to cut themselves off from it, or from the faith experience of ordinary believers that underlies it. The Church's ordinary theologians represent its 'front line' (Astley, 2002, p. 162) and 'the very foundation of its theologising' (Clark-King, 2004, p. 23).

Posture is another metaphor that may be used to mark out theology. The God-talk of ordinary theology frequently lies closer to the 'celebratory' style of worship, preaching and much of Scripture than it does to the more 'critical' theology that tests this language against standards of reason or orthodoxy, and probes its meaning and truth (Williams, 2000b, pp. xiii–xvi). The Roman Catholic theologian Hans Urs von Balthasar distinguished a kneeling theology, or 'theology at prayer', from the very different sort of theology that occurs when we sit down to reflect on our prayers – our 'theology at the desk' (von Balthasar, 1960, p. 224). The metaphorical posture of ordinary theology is the bent knee, halfway between prayer and study; it is best symbolized either as on its way down towards, or as rising up out of, prayer and worship. For ordinary theology is talking about God that keeps close to the stance of talking *to* God. It is often generated from the experience of worship, meditation or prayer, frequently in the midst of life, and easily leads us back into these experiences.

I would argue that this allows ordinary theology to be 'salvific' – in other words, to bring about wholeness, healing and salvation in the person who employs it. And that is why this sort of theology (all of it, or just a key part of it) 'works' for people. Unless our religious beliefs have this positive spiritual effect, we are unlikely to embrace them closely or for very long. If they do not help us find meaning in our lives and provide us with a secure anchor in the choppy seas and violent storms that batter us, we shall discover that we have ceased to hold on to them.

Ordinary theology also expresses and evokes our way of seeing the world, what has been called our 'onlook'. People say things like, 'I look on death as a gateway to a new life [or as the end of all that gives it meaning]'; 'I look on this disabled baby, or that difficult colleague at work, as a child of God [or as a useless burden]'; 'I look on the poor widow who puts her 50p into the collection plate as donating more than the rich banker in the next pew with his £50 note [or as making a trivial and pointless gesture].' Ordinary theology expresses *how we see* people, situations and behaviour.

Deep, motivating beliefs are not always explicitly expressed; for many people find this task too alien or at least too embarrassing. Hence many Christians don't often use the word 'God', even when they are talking about their faith. But, obviously, it is a lot easier to tell what people believe about God when they articulate their theological reflections in words. When it *is* expressed, as we have seen, the *style* of ordinary theology is usually more vivid, and often richer in story and figurative language, by comparison with the carefully qualified concepts and inferences of academic theology. It is also more 'bitty' – more 'bits-and-pieces' – than it is systematic; and it is more autobiographical, individual and personal than distanced and objective. Ordinary theology uses anecdotes, aphorisms and even clichés more than it employs reasoned arguments. It is even quite willing to apply concrete, human language to God – which is something we also find in the early chapters of Genesis and in many other places in the Bible. This may seem rather unsophisticated, but it can nevertheless convey some very profound theology, as the authors of Scripture also succeed in doing.

Here are some examples of this sort of God-talk, taken from interviews with ordinary theologians.

- 'I think Jesus is full of God.'
- 'I, in my mind, think of Jesus still as an outer limb of God.'
- 'I suppose if you look at it in terms of getting into a stadium, and God is giving out the tickets … You don't need to spend loads of money to get a ticket. In fact it is probably the more lowly person who is more guaranteed a place.'
- (This one is from a witty teenager, talking about the differences between the Old and New Testaments.) 'Perhaps God calmed down when he got a son.'
- And here is an example from Lee Hall's radio play about a terminally ill little girl, *Spoonface Steinberg* (first broadcast in 1997). She has just told the cleaning lady that she thinks she might have

caught her cancer from God; to which 'Mrs Spud' responds, 'If God's got cancer, we're all in trouble.' Indeed ...

TO DO

In your view, what valuable theological insights, if any, are expressed in these snippets of ordinary theology?

In contrast to these examples, you will find that academic theology's style is usually more dispassionate and impersonal, measured and prosaic; in particular, it is more likely to use technical concepts, and many more – and more complex – inferences and explanations. If they value their careers, academics must also show originality in their theology, which is a quality that is 'not what's looked for' in more ordinary discourse (Williams, 2000a, p. 75).

All theology is a matter of 'faith seeking understanding', as the eleventh-century theologian Anselm put it, adding, 'I believe, in order that I may understand.' Ordinary theology itself is certainly a 'reflective', 'thoughtful' or 'questioning' theology (Migliore, 2004, pp. 1–2). Thinking is not a monopoly of the university; but this critical aspect of theology is much more developed within academic theology. In *that* context:

> *Theology is the Christian faith subjected to critical thought.* This could be a disconcerting definition ... In our culture the word 'critical' usually means to find fault or to denigrate or to repudiate ... [But] a critic was a judge who was thought to be discerning, capable of making wise decisions ... because he operated with good criteria or standards of judgment. (Inbody, 2005, p. 14)

Ordinary theology, however, is less concerned with debating theology than with giving it *voice*. Continuing to employ metaphors, the voice of ordinary theology has a certain 'tone': it is a more direct expression of faith, and in using it people often arouse, strengthen and deepen faith in other people (as preachers are supposed to do) – and also within themselves. This ordinary theological voice frequently functions less as an exchange of information and more as a means of maintaining relationships. One might say – as others have said of much female speech – that it is a form of 'rapport' language as much as, or more than, a form of 'report' language; for it is often used for creating and expressing close, harmonious relationships with a shared understanding, rather than solely to communicate objective facts independent of those who embrace these facts. In these respects, the distinction between the voices of ordinary theology and academic theology is similar to the distinction made by the novelist Ursula Le Guin (Le Guin, 1989, pp. 147–51), between:

- the 'mother-tongue' of the home, which is the language of communication and relationship ('we learn it from our mothers and speak it to our kids');
- the 'father tongue' of disinterested, distanced analysis, objectivity and argument, which we need to go to college fully to learn.

However, the difference between *our* two types of language – the ordinary and the academic – is not just (or perhaps not at all) a difference between the sexes.

TO DO

Think of examples from your personal experience, when you or other people have used 'ordinary' or 'academic' language when thinking about God.

What are the strengths and weaknesses of each kind of language?

Who's listening?

Part of the difference between the more homely ordinary theology and its academic cousin lies in the differences between their *audiences*. It is often said that theology addresses three different 'publics':

- the Church;
- the academy – often meaning a university setting where people are engaged in the study of religion, rather than the development of Christian theology, and (less often);
- the 'public square' of society in general (cf. Tracy, 1981, ch. 1).

Those who read this book are likely to be most interested in the first of these audiences, and therefore most interested in the discourse in which the Church speaks to itself, using a 'communal voice' through which we articulate together our beliefs about the things of our faith. In this perspective, ordinary theology is not only an individual but also a communal thing: a choral performance as well as a solo. But note that, while such performances can produce the most beautiful and harmonious sounds, it is rare for the individuals that make up the choir all to be singing the same notes in unison. Rather, different groups (or individuals) will sing in 'parts', with these parts coming together to form a single harmony that depends on the differences between them. There is here a unity that incorporates diversity (and therefore individuality) – a 'one' that is created out of the 'many'.

We shall return to this theme in Chapters 3 and 9. For the moment, we may simply recognize the significance that this metaphor gives to variety, not only within theology's audience but in the different voices of a diverse Christian theology as well.

Variety of sources

We cannot ignore and should not seek to iron out this variety. The human activities that make up both ordinary and academic theology are too varied for that, and this variation is too important. Although the underlying landscapes (subjects, topics, content) remain the same, theologians can – and frequently do! – differ radically as to how they survey and map this agreed terrain. Disagreement among academic theologians is perhaps as common as disagreement within Christianity itself, particularly with regard to what they take to be important in the Christian faith, as well as how these things should be expressed.

These differences in the content of theology often reflect different views of the relative authority that ought to be given to different *sources* of theology: those significant torrents and waterfalls located in the religious highlands, which eventually flow down into and together constitute the broad theological river of the plain. These sources include:

- the Bible;
- the traditions of the Church (particularly its worship and teachings);
- reason (particularly as expressed in the thinking of present-day theologians);
- the religious experience of individuals and of the wider Church;
- the contemporary culture.

We shall explore in more detail questions about experience in Chapter 4, and questions about the authority of the Bible and the Church's tradition in Chapter 5, concentrating here on some of the other sources of – or 'formative factors' in – the creation of theology (see Macquarrie, 1977, pp. 4–18). Before we do this, however, please reflect on how you might answer the following questions.

TO DO

Which of the sources listed above are the more important ones *for you*, and why?

To what extent should Christian theology be influenced by our contemporary values and ways of thinking? What is the advantage of this? What are the dangers?

To 'reveal' is to 'unveil' something – to disclose to someone a meaning or a reality that would otherwise be hidden from them. Some ideas within Christianity may be entirely human, in the sense that they derive from the activity of human minds alone. However, Christians hold that much Christian truth has been in some way revealed by God, usually through God's original, 'primordial' or 'classic' disclosure to the people of Israel and especially to the followers of Jesus. Either directly or indirectly this is God's speech, *God's talk*.

Revelation may be understood in two different ways:

1 As a revelation of *truths* about God: that is, of *God's own claims* about himself ('Godself'), made directly to human minds.
2 Or as a revelation of *God Godself*, chiefly of God's character, revealed through God's action in history (principally in the history of Israel and in the life, death and resurrection of Jesus), which is subsequently represented in an (indirect) *account by human beings*.

Whichever route it comes by, revelation begins in an event, an act in which God takes the initiative; and it ends in language that can be understood by human beings.

In version (1), however, which is the idea of a *propositional* or *verbal revelation*, God tells us about Godself by revealing statements of theology directly. The content of revelation is here a set of truths or statements about God's nature or intention. 'The word of the LORD came to me saying ...' is how the Old Testament prophets understood this event (e.g. Jeremiah 1.1–10; 2.1–3; Ezekiel 6.1, etc.; cf. Isaiah 20.2–4). Paul sometimes seems to be saying something similar (e.g. 1 Corinthians 7.10; 11.23).

It is tempting to view this model of revelation as a sort of 'hearing', although it involves some 'inner sense' instead of our ordinary sense organs (and is sometimes 'seen' – cf. Isaiah 1.1; 2.1). In whatever way it is conveyed to people, however, this is a form of religious communication that arrives already expressed in words. And according to John Calvin (see Chapter 8), in revelation God 'adjusts' and 'descends' to our capacities, 'accommodating' his revelation to our limited understanding.

> At best, he thought, God speaks baby talk to us because of our limitations. We should always be aware, therefore, that revelation does not mean utter and thorough explanation, but it is accommodated to particular places, cultures, languages, translations, and concepts. There were places where the Israelites had a dramatic understanding of God, and there were places where they pretty clearly did not grasp the way God is later understood in light of the revelation in Jesus Christ. For example, polygamy ... and holy war [were] thought to be consistent with the will of God in some of the Old Testament ... It is difficult to conclude that what happened is that God changed; rather, what it looks like is that the *understanding* of God changed and developed over the course of time. This is the meaning of progressive revelation. (Stiver, 2009, p. 92)

But is this how revelation really, or always, works? On version (2) above, sometimes called the *non-propositional* view of revelation, what is revealed are not any words or truths about God but God's own nature, activity or presence. God is revealed as the God of judgement and love, in and through events of the 'salvation history' of the Old and New Testaments – in the exodus from Egypt, the struggles for justice for the poor within Israel and pre-eminently in Jesus. Such events reveal the activity and the character of God as people 'saw in them' – or 'looked on' them or 'saw them as' (see pp. 7–8 and 34–6) – the grace and demand of the Almighty. But on this view, the theology that clothes these revelations is not itself God's direct word. It is, rather, composed from human reflections on the events, including descriptions of the kind of God whom people 'perceived' as acting behind and within these historical events.[1]

---

1 On another view of revelation, God may be said to supervise or authorize a person's actual writing or speaking, giving their words – which are the creation of human beings – a divine authority and function as 'God's words': rather as a senior official or manager does, when signing a letter or issuing a report that has been written 'in his/her name' by other people. See Astley, 2004, p. 34.

We should say a little more about the nature of the experience that receives, and sometimes interprets, this divine revelation. Revelation is always *God's gift*. On our second interpretation, it is human beings who give this revelation its words. But even with the first type of (propositional) revelation, experience plays its part. Those who received such revelations may have been more passive, but they must have had some experience for it to be true that God had revealed Godself at all. However much I insist on disrobing in front of you, if you avert your eyes or leave the room, there will be no disclosure. (And a good job, too, in this case.) God gives, but we must be open to receive what God gives, or there will be no communication and nothing will ever be revealed. More generally, 'the Christian faith cannot be apprehended as true until the experience of the believer appropriates it as true' (Inbody, 2005, p. 52). Even those who take the highest view of revelation claim that this affirmative response is crucial in the process of revelation, although they often insist that it is only by the enlightenment or *inward testimony of the Holy Spirit* that humans are convinced that this revelation came to us, as Calvin says, 'by the instrumentality of men, from the very mouth of God'.

While some theologians lay more stress on the divine initiative in revelation, and others on the contribution made by the human response, both are necessary.

Another significant division within theology lies in the importance theologians give not to human experience but to human reason. Again, some will stress the divine side at the expense of the human – arguing that our reason is just wholly inadequate to comprehend the saving truths of God: for some because human reason has become corrupted by sin, for others because it could never have had such power. This is quite an extreme position, and many have reacted strongly against it, arguing that our reason may properly be a formative factor in our theology. In other words, our theology is partly formed by our reasoning about God, and even about God's revelation.

As we saw above, although this activity is often described as 'critical' reason this does not mean that the thinking involved is negative or destructive. In this context, 'critical' simply means 'evaluative'; critical reason makes assessments or judgements about the faults and merits of some claim, on the basis of arguments and evidence. Critical reason is always involved in elucidating something (analysing and exploring it, making its meaning clear); only sometimes does it amend and correct theology in order to help make it more reasonable. But on occasions this is precisely what our theology needs.

And note that 'reasonable' is the right word here, implying that theology is *scrutinized and supported* by reason. The rather similar word, 'rational', is normally used only for forms of theology that are *founded* solely on human argument (sometimes called 'natural theology'), and not on God's revelation or the religious experience of human beings.

Sometimes reason is given a wholly pivotal role in determining the nature of Christian theology. At the end of the seventeenth century, the English philosopher John Locke argued that, as 'reason must be our last judge and guide in everything', even revelation needs to be tested by it. (He had a rather limited view of the support that reason gives, understanding it in terms of revelation being accompanied by the evidence of 'outward signs' of miracles and fulfilled prophecies.) Locke's position will probably seem too extreme to most Christians. In a world like ours, however, where we are confronted by many sacred texts and conflicting claims to divine truth, many Christians would argue that we really have to exercise our reason in order to assess whether or not any one of them is likely to be a true revelation of God.

TO DO

How far would you say that your beliefs about God are reasonable? What do you mean by this?

Should appeals to divine revelation be subject to our fallible human judgement?

Culture and Christianity

Culture lies close to reason, in the sense that both are essentially human elements, and because in order to be understood – and to seem 'reasonable' – revelation must speak to the current intellectual and social climate of the times. 'If theology is to be intelligible, it has to use the language of the culture within which it is undertaken' (Macquarrie, 1977, p. 13).

In Chapter 1, I described the relationship between the reflections of the academic theologian and those of the more ordinary believer as a 'conversation'. This is a much used metaphor in theological circles. Another important theological interaction that is described in this way is that between the Christian faith and our human culture. ('Culture' being the shorthand for a society's normal ways of thinking and valuing, and the institutions and artefacts – including art, architecture and music – that expresses these ways.)

The German-American Protestant theologian Paul Tillich described the task of modern theology as involving *correlation*: that is, a mutual relationship or connection of interdependence between faith and culture. In Tillich's view, the cultural situation generates the 'ultimate questions' of human concern to which the sources of theology must give an answer, by 'speaking to culture' and often reconstructing belief in response to it. So 'theology moves back and forth between two poles, the eternal truth of its foundation and the temporal situation in which the eternal truth must be received' (Tillich, 1968, p. 3). But if this is so, then our culture really serves as a *source* for our theology, because 'the "questions" by which tradition is interpreted always reflect particular interests and ideological biases' (of our particular cultural situation) (Hodgson, 1994, p. 25).

Christian disbelief

The New Testament includes the injunction *not* to 'believe every spirit', but rather to 'test the spirits to see whether they are from God' (1 John 4.1). This echoes a common warning in the Bible against false prophecy (see Jeremiah 23.25–32; Mark 13.21–22; cf. 1 Kings 22). The 'commission to test the spirits' is interpreted by Christopher Morse as the critical dimension of Christian theology, which he understands as its 'task of faithful disbelief' (Morse, 2009, p. 14). (Note that adjective, 'faithful'.) Morse suggests ten 'tests of doctrinal faithfulness' and 'rubrics of accountability' by which the theologian should test any piece of theology:

> With the biblical witness as confirmed in the ongoing community of faith providing the orientation for their theological task of testing, Christian churches ask specific questions in seeking to recognize when faithfulness requires that some spirit of the times be disbelieved. Is the claim being made continuous with what is apostolic in the tradition? Is it congruent with what the Word of God in Scripture is speaking? Is it consistent with the community's prayer and worship? Is it truly catholic, that is, true for the church everywhere and not just in one place? Is it consonant with experience; that is, does it ring true to life in faith? Is it in keeping with a good conscience? What are the effects or consequences? Is the spirit that is being advocated pertinent to, or an evasion of, what is crucial, what matters most, in the situation at hand? Is it coherent in relation to contemporary modes of thought? How comprehensive is the particular teaching with respect to the full range of Christian confession? (Morse, 2009, p. 45)

TO DO

In your view, which of these tests should have a greater priority, and why?

What should we do when the results of these tests disagree?

Further reading

Astley, J., 2002, *Ordinary Theology: Looking Listening and Learning in Theology*, Aldershot: Ashgate, Ch. 3.

Astley, J. and Christie, A., 2006, *Taking Ordinary Theology Seriously*, Cambridge: Grove Books.

Dulles, A., 1992, *Models of Revelation*, Maryknoll, NY: Orbis Books.

McGrath, A. E., 2007, *Christian Theology: An Introduction*, Oxford: Blackwell, Chs 6 and 7.

McGrath, A. E., 2008, *Theology: The Basics*, Oxford: Blackwell, 'Getting Started' and ch. 1.

Migliore, D. L., 2004, *Faith Seeking Understanding: An Introduction to Christian Theology*, Grand Rapids, MI: Eerdmans, Ch. 2.

Morse, C., 2009, *Not Every Spirit: A Dogmatics of Christian Belief*, New York: Continuum, Part 1.

3

Doing Theology and Studying Theology

What does it mean to 'do theology' or to say that you are a 'theologian', whether an ordinary theologian or an academic one?

The sophisticated question to ask a new undergraduate student is, 'What are you reading?', hoping that the answer isn't, 'I'm still on the last Harry Potter book' (though that's a lot better than the first Beatrix Potter book). So there are different types or depths of reading. But in most subject areas, people don't usually talk about *doing* a subject rather than just *studying* (or 'reading') it.

Yet the distinction is sometimes drawn between simply reading about a subject and being actively engaged with and in it. To 'be' a scientist involves observation and experiment, employing the 'scientific method' of interrogating the world and thinking scientifically about it. To encourage this, science students have to do practical work or field work. Science is learned 'first hand', as well as from books and lectures. It is not enough simply to fill your head with the facts and explanations that proper scientists have proposed or discovered. It is not enough just to believe *that* scientific theories are true. In some sense, you have also to 'believe in' science and act accordingly. Real scientists live science.

However, you don't need to be a novelist to study novels; and you certainly don't need to be a child in order to study children's psychology (it helps if you are not). So do you really need to be a *believer* before you can 'study God'? Do you need to talk *to* God, through prayer or confession or worship, in order to talk *about* God? Do we need to *live* Christianity in order to understand it?

TO DO

What reasons can you think of for (a) agreeing with, and (b) disagreeing with, these three questions?

At one level, the answer to all these questions must be 'no'. If you look at introductory textbooks in Christian theology or doctrine, you will usually find a (sometimes half-hearted) justification for a sort of non-vocational, *academic theology for non-believers*. If theology is essentially something like 'thinking about questions raised by and about the religions' (Ford, 2013, p. 14), then theology can be studied by secular as well as religious students. People *can* study Christian ideas without being believers. And they can 'do' it too, if doing theology only means taking it sufficiently seriously, by exploring and assessing Christian beliefs. If that is all that the phrase 'doing theology' labels, then it only involves exercising certain general thinking skills to which you are committed, and reflecting on texts and evidence with some general tools of study that you have come to rely on and trust (believe in?) (see Chapter 6). This, after all, seems to be all that is involved in doing history or doing geography and so on. In which case, we may agree that 'the prime task of theology is that of understanding', and that the theologian 'is not primarily concerned ... to deepen faith or to defend a gospel' (Hebblethwaite, 1980, p. 21). We might even say that such real theologians 'live' the quest for theological understanding.

But, as Mark McIntosh argues, even the best students – and even ourselves – 'will never really see what theology is about until and unless we recognize that true theologians see everything from this new perspective, from this sharing in the dying and rising of Jesus' (McIntosh, 2008, p. 18). And even the non-religious students should acknowledge that 'theology comes to birth because of [the Christian communities'] ongoing encounter with God' (p. 13). If students can't see that, they will never 'get it': they will never understand what the point of a theology is *for the people who own it*.

As these communities are seeking 'to think about everything from God's point of view', McIntosh can even say that 'thinking theologically ... might be said to be an undergoing of the divine', which is a matter of allowing 'one's own thinking to be addressed and shaped by the divine thinking' (pp. 36–7). While you won't become personally warmer through studying the laws of thermodynamics, and you won't develop a friendship with Jeff Astley just by reading this book (*however* much you paid for it), studying theology *can* 'improve the level of communication and interaction' between the student and God (p. 15). Doing theology in this way may even be a knowing of God that 'includes knowing that one is comprehensively known by God' (Ford, 2013, p. 157). To which we can only respond, 'Gosh'.

TO DO

Reflect on the differences between knowing God, knowing about God and being known by God.

If theology can work like this, then our simple distinction between studying theology and doing theology will need qualifying. Doing theology *as a Christian believer* might then seem to be different from doing theology as a good student *of* theology. Doing theology as a believer, as someone who has and owns a theology, won't necessarily make you a better student. But it sounds as though it might have the potential to make you 'better' at being a Christian. This seems to be a deeper sense of 'understanding theology', including the theology in Scripture:

> The goal of Scripture ... is understanding at an intuitive, embodied level. This does not rule out factual knowledge and even propositional knowledge. It presupposes ... a stage of criticism and examination ... [Yet] Scripture, in a sense, is not understood until it reaches the stage of appropriation ... the level of transformation of our way of living in the world. (Stiver, 2009, pp. 75–6)

The really important exercise *for Christian believers* engaged in doing theology is that they *interact* with this material, 'so as to produce a theology that they can believe in and live by' (Astley, 2010, p. 8). And if *that* is the goal, then no one can do that sort of theology for you. You cannot copy such a theology from a book or by looking over someone else's shoulder (even shoulders on the Internet). You have to do it for yourself. This is, I guess, another aspect of faith seeking understanding (see Chapter 2). It is the Christian faith seeking *my* understanding, and my response. And, thus, it is also my faith seeking understanding. It is thinking *for oneself* about God, certainly. And it is *taking responsibility* for one's own Christian beliefs: for what one really believes as a Christian (Cobb, 1994, pp. 17–18).

'Learning theology', then, or 'learning God', is now not just a matter of 'learning about' these things. While doing theology for oneself may, and often should, involve studying the results of other people's theological reflection and expression, it also involves *doing your own theology*; indeed, it involves 'doing God' – and in a very personal way.

This time it's personal

'Personal' here does not mean 'on your own'. Indeed, many Christians would argue that we should avoid making Christian belief too individualistic a thing. It is the Church that believes, and individuals believe only as part of the Church. And sometimes it can seem that we have to leave it to the Church to do our believing for us. So some worshippers may even lapse into silence at the bits of creeds or hymns that they cannot fully endorse, allowing (the rest of) the Church to fill in the gaps.

I am concerned, however, that it can sometimes be too easy to abdicate responsibility for our own believing to other people, whether the others are our family or culture, our congregation or denomination – or the whole Church. As we saw in Chapter 2, the individual voice is an essential part of the choir, and the harmonies of the one choral performance require these individual (and different) voices.

The Church boasts two ancient species of 'rules of faith' or *creeds*. The earliest form is most clearly based on the confession of faith required of a candidate for baptism. Initially, baptism included a set of questions ('Do you believe in God the Father ...' etc.). But centuries later these transformed into an individual confession of faith ('*I* believe in God the Father ...' etc.) – as we still have it, in what has become known as 'the Apostles' Creed'. Some version of this individual, 'I believe', creed is regularly used today, especially within Anglican and Protestant worship.

But many Christians will be more familiar with a creed that begins rather differently. Some of the great theological debates of the councils of the early Church were resolved in the reformulation of baptismal creeds as 'conciliar' (that is, council) creeds that routinely began '*We* believe ...' The so-called 'Nicene Creed', which is associated not so much with the Council of Nicaea (325) but with the Councils at Constantinople (381) and Chalcedon (451), is the most important of these. It has become the most widely used creed of the Christian Church, and is regularly said or sung in the eucharistic liturgy ('Holy Communion' or 'Mass') of most churches.

Christian belief, then, is both individual ('I') and corporate ('we'). But in both cases it is personal.

Ordinary and academic theology in conversation

I want now to develop this theme further. When we come to study theology in any academic context, we bring with us our own theology, which is usually quite ordinary in my sense of being innocent of and untouched by extraordinary, academic theological study. This is the right starting point. 'The only place that authentic theology can begin is with the real beliefs of real Christians ... We can grow daily only if we discover for ourselves that our beliefs are not adequate or appropriate' (Cobb, 1994, p. 41). (Or, I would add, if we discover that they are.)

No one enters into the task of theological learning, understanding or interpretation with empty minds or impassive hearts. Rather, we all approach the 'other' (including religious texts) 'with a mind that already contains our own ideas, set in the perspective of our own "viewpoint" or "standpoint", and with a heart infused with our own feelings, values and concerns' (Astley, 2010, p. 9). On this view, we are neither blank sheets of paper resting in the input tray of a printer, nor blank computer screens with their cursors passively marking time until prompted by someone else's input of information. In our case, there is some text there already.

Although people often speak of 'receiving' traditional religious teaching or insights from academic theology, this 'reception' is not like filling an empty jug at the tap. Nor, despite Isaiah 45.9; Jeremiah 18.1–8 and Romans 9.19–24, is it quite the same as moulding an unformed lump of clay on a potter's wheel (with one eye on a photograph of an ideal jug, or an 'ideal theologian', in order to serve as a model). It is more like chipping at a great tree trunk that already possesses a particular form or shape, modifying and transforming it in such a way that the wood comes to express something else *as well*: for example, the image of Mary standing over the slain body of her son. (Visit Durham Cathedral if you want to see the sculpture by local artist Fenwick Lawson, which is pictured overleaf.)

As I argued in Chapter 1, in learning theology by doing theology we enter into a metaphorical *conversation*: a developing theological dialogue between our own theology (initially our own *ordinary* theology) and the more academic theological resources offered by teachers, books and other students. In this interchange, what *we* think and what we already are always matters. After all, in the end we can only believe what *we* can believe. And, as the experts on the art and science of interpretation (or 'hermeneutics') insist, we cannot even understand the Christian tradition itself except through the lens of our present reflections.

In this learning conversation between our present ordinary theology and the academic theology we are studying, either partner may be the dominant voice. But, if this is a real (if metaphorical) discussion, conversation or dialogue, then the Bible and the Church must 'speak' – but so must we. For if we don't, then we won't *change* and we shall not, therefore, truly learn from them.

© Dr Fenwick Lawson, ARCA, DLitt (honoris causa) 1984
© Howard Little, BIPP 2004
(See http://stcuthbertsfinaljourney.com/2013/03/17/pieta-by-fenwick-lawson-unique-insights-from-his-daughter/)

Learning always involves change – even in theology! So, as the ideas we learn interact with our own ideas, the two will eventually coalesce and together transmute into something that may be rather different from either – and in a way that is often quite individual and personal. Like a conversation.

TO DO

Reflect on your own experience of reading or studying theology. In what ways are your own theological ideas responding to, and interacting with, the ideas in the material you are studying?

What does this experience feel like?

Critical theology

In Chapter 2 we reflected on the role that reason can play in the development of theology. I want to explore that theme further here. Theological education, understood as a species of adult Christian education, needs to be both *formative* and *critical* (Astley, 1994, ch. 5; 2000, ch. 2). It must therefore combine:

1 the formation of learners in Christian beliefs, attitudes, emotions, skills, and dispositions to act and experience;
2 extending their evaluative thinking, so as to help them examine and assess the Christian tradition from their own perspective.

This combination is required both for the students' own sakes and for the good of the whole Church. For only by combining formation and evaluation can people do theology for themselves, as they learn to think for themselves about their faith. To quote John Cobb yet again:

> The effort to determine what you really believe – that is, the beliefs that shape your life – [already] involves reason. Questioning the

sources [of these beliefs] is a rational activity, as is every stage in the process of answering ... Reason is involved in attributing authority to tradition and Scripture and determining how they function as authorities ... [and] in the development of the content of Scripture and tradition ... Every interpretation of Scripture and tradition is [also] an act of reason ... [Reason] is your creativity coming to deeper understanding, more clarity and greater comprehensiveness. (Cobb, 1993, pp. 64–5)

Hence, as I have put it:

although I am the first to claim that reason is not at the heart of religion, in the sense of its deepest motivation and foundation, this does not mean that it can be cavalierly sidelined. Hard thinking must always be a central strand of adult faith, as it is central to being an adult. (Astley, 2007, p. xii)

TO DO

When has critical thinking caused you to change your mind on a religious issue?

Many would argue that there is no alternative option, for this reason (sorry): that criticism is essentially 'judgement', 'assessment' or 'evaluation', and because we dare not slough off our responsibility not only for using these skills in appraising Christianity *as true*, but also for judging it – in this particular text, interpretation, hymn, chorus song, or other activity – *to be Christian*.

Truly Christian congregations are continually engaged in critical reflection on their own faithfulness to the Christian norm of meeting and worshipping 'in Jesus' name'. Congregations are in this way 'constituted by a practice that is inherently self-critical' (Kelsey, 1992, p. 187). Christians should always be asking themselves, 'Is this truly Christian – this thought of mine, this action of mine, this sermon of mine?' 'Is this really of Christ?' 'Is it – am I – faithful to

Jesus' name?' Critical theological reflection, at its best, gives us the tools to make these fundamentally *theological* judgements, without which the Church cannot be Christ's Church and our gospel cannot be his gospel. This, surely, is part of the 'testing of the spirits' that we explored in the last chapter.

On being a humble student

This subheading may make your hackles rise even further. After all, academic scholarship often appears arrogant and domineering. And humility is a character trait that doesn't get a particularly enthusiastic press these days. But I want to argue that, deep down, all scholars and all study require a certain stance towards the other. It is the stance of *humble listening*.

Although listening is often presented as an activity or a skill, both of these are undergirded by a fundamental attitude or demeanour. Listening is universally recognized – at least in principle – as central to human love in general and pastoral care in particular. It should therefore already lie at the heart of the Christian, and the Christian minister's, calling. Listening betokens respect – and more. 'Listening is that crucial act of love for which human beings long. With careful listening come the gifts of being heard, known, understood' (Moschella, 2008, p. 254).

The attitude of listening is central to learning as well. The French thinker Simone Weil (1909–43) wrote of 'attention' – by which she meant an expectant, non-seeking and non-striving attentiveness – as something that is central to prayer and worship, as well as to pastoral care (for 'those who are unhappy have no need for anything in this world but people capable of giving them their attention'). But attention is also, Weil argued, at the heart of academic study. It is this stance that allowed her to claim that study is 'like a sacrament'. It is a waiting on truth out of a deep desire whose fulfilment releases the joy of learning. In every exercise of learning:

> there is a special way of waiting upon truth, setting our hearts upon it ... giving our attention to the data of a problem ...

> Studies are nearer to God because of the attention which is their soul. Whoever goes through years of study without developing this attention within himself has lost a great treasure. (Weil, 1977, pp. 50–1)

Attention, for Weil, is the substance of our love of God, our love of neighbour and our love of study.

It has been said that 'listening is difficult because it requires us to give up the role of expert, and become a learner again' (Moschella, 2008, p. 142). Within the Christian frame, we might say that this involves becoming a disciple again. In the New Testament, the disciple, the *mathetes*, is the 'one who directs his mind'. She or he is the apprentice who learns the truth 'in the authentic Jesus-way' (in Leslie Houlden's phrase). The disciple is formed by Christ the master through following, imitating, listening to and learning Christ, 'on the way'. Christians must never cease to do this and to be this, even – especially – when they are busy with the study of theology.

There is a proper humility in this demeanour of listening that is also essential in academic study. Such humility, however, is quite compatible with an equally proper pride in our learning. Humility is only a virtue as a middle way between two vices – on the one hand, arrogance ('I know it all already; you have nothing to teach me that I need to learn'); on the other – equally bad – utter self-abnegation ('I am nothing; I'll never understand this'). Humility is a much more *realistic* stance for living. It involves being realistic about our gifts and knowledge, and about how much we need to learn and how little we honestly understand.

It is required in particular in theology, if theology is not just 'talk about God' but also (however feebly and humanly) 'divine teaching'. And it is especially relevant as and when we discover that we don't just have or invent these ideas, this theology. Rather, we find that the ideas 'have us' (as McIntosh says) – that is, they hold us. And they may also challenge us, bringing us into a new place, transforming us. If this is all true, then we must be humble in our learning of theology.

TO DO

How do you respond to these claims about the spiritual character that is required for the study of theology: are they overblown or underdone?

Can you suggest other attitudes and virtues that might assist us in our theological study?

Further reading

Astley, J., 2010, *SCM Studyguide to Christian Doctrine*, London: SCM Press, Ch. 1.

Astley, J. and Francis, L. J. (eds), 2013, *Exploring Ordinary Theology: Everyday Christian Believing and the Church*, Farnham: Ashgate, Ch. 5.

McIntosh, M. A., 2008, *Divine Teaching: An Introduction to Christian Theology*, Oxford: Blackwell, Part I.

Migliore, D. L., 2004, *Faith Seeking Understanding: An Introduction to Christian Theology*, Grand Rapids, MI: Eerdmans, Ch. 1.

Pattison, G., 1998, *The End of Theology and the Task of Thinking about God*, London: SCM Press, Ch. 1.

4

Locating Theology at the Centre: Experience, Belief, Faith and Practice

The language of theology is primarily the language of belief. A theology – whether it is owned by Paul, Luther, the Pope or yourself – involves believing certain things ('claims', 'truths', 'facts') about God, including things about God's relationship to creation, chiefly God's human creation (us), and about God's agents of salvation, in particular Jesus and the Church.

But what is involved in believing something; and how does religious believing relate to other parts of our lives, such as what we experience and how we feel, what we do and who we are?

TO DO

Below is one (oversimple) attempt to represent the relationship between three different areas of our life. In what ways does the diagram reflect how these things relate together, and which parts of it do not fit the way things seem to you?

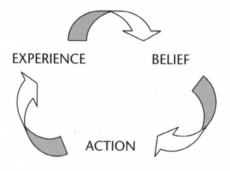

EXPERIENCE   BELIEF

ACTION

There are many ways in which this diagram could be amended:

- Our beliefs, to some extent, determine our interpretations of experience, so we could add a second arrow between these two areas pointing the other way.
- Experience doesn't always directly arise from actions that originate in us. Often we are passive or only responsive, while the world – including other people – acts on us.
- There is a category that underlies all three areas of the diagram, and is made up of our character, spirituality, moral values, religious stances, tendencies to act, orientations to the world and to other people, and so on. This is the category of ATTITUDES, which we may think of as more fundamental than, and giving rise to, our beliefs and actions (Evans, 1979), and as informing our experiences.
- FEELINGS are key components of both attitudes and emotions, and they usually accompany our experiences (see below), our beliefs and our actions very closely, giving them a particular, affective 'taste' or 'colour'.

Experience: can you see it yet?

Experience is generally regarded as a good thing. Employers often reject job applications from people who don't have enough of it. It is what distinguishes those who have only read about a place or a person, or seen them on television, from the more fortunate (or unfortunate?) folk who have actually met this man or woman or visited that city 'in person' – those who have *encountered* them and are *acquainted* with them. Experience is something you cannot have at second hand; you have to undergo it for yourself. Experience leaves an 'impression' on you and often stirs your feelings in a unique way.

As a noun and particularly as a verb, however, the word is often applied simply to feeling something or having certain emotions. We may call these 'subjective experiences', to distinguish them from the 'objective' experiences described above. There is often a connection between the two. In particular, objective experiences of the presence and activity of God will most likely give rise to subjective experiences such as awe, guilt, comfort, love or acceptance.

But does the category of objective experience apply within religion? Well, 'no one has ever seen God' (John 1.18), although the Bible hints at some partial – and always very mysterious – *theophanies* or 'showings' of God (e.g. Exodus 33.18–23; Isaiah 6.1–5). Some Christians have also claimed to have 'seen', after some fashion, angels or saints, especially the Virgin Mary, and even Christ. Mostly, however, 'religious experience' is expressed – certainly in the Bible – on the model of hearing, rather than seeing. As we noted in Chapter 2, the prophet declares that 'the *word* of the LORD came to me, saying ...'.

TO DO

Read Exodus 3.1–6; 33.7–23; Isaiah 6.1–8; 22.14; Ezekiel 10; Hosea 1.1–2; Revelation 1.1–3 and chapter 4. How do you interpret these texts? What sort of experience might lie behind them? What claims do they make about the relationship between the prophet and God?

Of course, God, God's word and many other 'objects' of religious experience are not things within the world of space and time. So this sort of experience cannot be a matter of seeing or hearing (or touching, tasting, etc.) in any literal way. Such language is being used here metaphorically, in an attempt to describe a more private, mysterious and spiritual way of perceiving God or of sensing God's demands, promises and intentions (see Chapter 7).

There is, however, a further kind of religious vision or spiritual 'seeing' that is rather more common. We may call it spiritual or theological *imagination*. The English noun 'imagination' is usually used of having ideas, and specifically of being creative and resourceful. But it comes from the Latin word, *imaginare* – to 'picture to oneself' – and this can be said to include discerning connections and so gaining insight. In particular, it may involve perceiving, recognizing and seeing something *as* being something else as well, by looking on it in a certain way.

This is something we do all the time. We 'recognize' this bird as a kestrel or that face as our friend; we 'view' some life event as a challenge or a 'wake-up call'. Or we hear 'my favourite song' – not just some notes in sequence, or 'my child's voice' – not just some anonymous speech. This process involves *interpretation*, of course. But we don't see or hear something and then later on – away from the experience – *infer* the presence of our child or of a kestrel as the best explanation of the experience we have had. The recognition we are thinking about here does not depend on reasoning in that sort of way; it doesn't involve our 'discursive thinking'. It is more 'immediate' than that (for it is not mediated by concepts or arguments), and more 'intuitive' – more like a perception than an argument.

It is the same with much religious experience (see Hick, 2008, ch. 2). It is not that people see the world, or other people, or the history of Israel, and then *argue to* God's presence and purpose from these observable facts, as an *explanation* of them. Rather, people 'see' or 'find' God *in and through them*. They experience *as*: seeing the world as God's world and other people as God's children; and themselves as sinners, healed and forgiven by God's grace. Jesus taught us to do that – to see things through his eyes. He saw this damaged or sinful person as a child of God, and this impoverished widow at the Temple treasury as someone who gives more than all those rich donors. Christians are not only people who look on and hear about the teachings, life, death and resurrection of Jesus. They are people who also experience these things *as* God's word, God's Kingdom, God's presence and God's love. And they see Jesus as their Lord. Recalling the portrayal of ordinary theology in Chapter 2, we may call this our Christian 'onlook' on things (see pp. 7–8).

People often say that spiritual perception or religious insight and experience are more about wisdom than intellectual cleverness. Wisdom derives from an Old English root, *weid*, 'to see', and has been defined as 'an insightful seeing or envisioning of what shows or presents itself' (Hodgson, 1999, p. 7). The word 'insightful' suggests a sort of wise perception. 'Beware', writes David Ford, 'of any pursuit of theological information and knowledge that is not somehow in the service of wisdom' (Ford, 2013, p. 166). We have been warned!

So what sort of imagination, what species of vision, does a Christian theologian require? In a word, she or he needs *to see with the eyes of faith*. And faith, according to Mark McIntosh, is 'the means of divine teaching that allows theologians ... to begin to see things as God does, to understand things by means of God's ideas about them' (McIntosh, 2008, p. 28). It requires us to begin to see things – and eventually to see everything – from a new, gospel perspective.

> Vision is a key word throughout religion. I think of this vision as a new take on what has always been before us ... a *re*vision of everyday experience.
>
> To be converted is, in the end, not so much a matter of seeing different things, as of seeing the same things differently. It involves seeing this child, woman or man – or this slice of the natural world or sliver of historical time – *as* holy, as sacred, as God's. Seeing life as a spiritual journey is not really about seeing something else, something *additional* ...
>
> If faith is not based on some additional experience, something added to our day-to-day experience, we must think about it in terms of seeing more clearly and in more depth something that is already and always there. Something like the meaning of life or the hand of God. (Astley, 2007, pp. 5–6)

TO DO

What are the strengths and weaknesses of understanding faith as a way of seeing?

One aspect of this form of religious experience is discerning what is of religious, spiritual and theological *value* and *importance*. It is possible to study theology in such a way that we completely miss the point of it. We can fail to see what theology is really all about if we lack the wisdom and insight to get to the heart of it, and see the point and purpose and value of what it is talking about.

I repeat, theology will come alive for us only as we 'get it'; and part of that 'getting' involves theology becoming redemptive for us. Unless we properly value the things of God, we shall never really see the point of them, never understand them. And unless people want the Kingdom of God, they will be blind to its possibility, presence and saving power.

Another element in religious perception is *seeing connections*. And a large part of that is spotting similarities, likenesses and relevancies. I shall never pick up the pearl of real worth from the storehouse of the Christian tradition, unless I both discern its value *and* see that it meets my needs and will fit perfectly into my crown. In less figurative language, I won't begin a conversation with you unless I both value you *and* discern that you have something to say to me, something that is of relevance to me (even if it is about you).

A very similar thing is required if people are going to reflect theologically on their experience or their life. Taking up the terminology of Paul Tillich and others (see p. 17), practical theologians often write about 'correlating' or 'connecting' (a) human experience and practice, to (b) the Scriptures and the theological and moral insights of the Christian tradition. 'Only connect!' as E. M. Forster said, in writing of prose and passion. In other words, see the theological point and connect it to your own thinking, feeling and living. In most theology, 'insight is obtained by seeing how things are connected' (Hodgson, 1994, p. 16).

Yet there often seems to be a great distance between my world and the world described by theology. Perhaps the gap between the two is best leaped by the imagination with the aid of figures of speech. Jesus seems to have thought so, when in his parable-stories he made connections between everyday things and situations, on the one hand, and what God *means* – who God *is* – on the other (see Chapter 7). He particularly taught what it would mean if God were really to be in charge, if his will *is* 'done on earth as it is in heaven'; if his Kingdom really came (see Borg, 2003, ch. 7).

As Christian disciples and theologians, we need to make – to 'see' – our own sort of connections. We need to ask ourselves, 'What is my life *like*?' And then look hard to see if anything in our experience resonates, or 'chimes in', with anything in Christian Scripture, worship or doctrine. Can we connect them together?

TO DO

Try this exercise yourself.

1 Select a concern in your everyday life.
2 Think of a story or image from a novel, film or other work of (low or high) art that is in some way *like* this issue and can illuminate it.
3 Enter that 'imaginary world' and explore how things feel and look from within its perspective.
4 Try to seek out and spot some Bible story, hymn, prayer or insight within theology that echoes these images, feelings and perspectives.
5 Finally, ask what this bit of God-talk 'says' to the topic of your concern, and how you would reply to it from your own experience. Then let the conversation develop ...

(This task is easier than it sounds! Stages (2) and (3) are only there to help bridge the gap between your life and the Christian tradition; if they don't help, attempt the exercise without them, by moving directly from your concerns to some biblical or Christian text and idea that speaks to them.)

Belief: 'You don't believe that, do you?'

Christian theology is often understood, for example by Clement of Alexandria (*c.* 150–215), as 'Christian truth claims about God'. Our word 'creed' comes from the Latin verb 'to believe'. Christian theology seems to be all about exploring Christian beliefs.

Beliefs are, of course, important outside theology, too. Philosophers regard beliefs as comprising two elements:

- mental (or 'cognitive') states of holding something to be true, and being disposed to behave appropriately – to 'act on this belief';
- mental acts of 'assenting' to this belief.

The first, 'dispositional' dimension means that if you say that you believe that fire will burn you, I should expect you to tend to avoid touching live flames and to be willing to buy a fireguard in order to keep the children away from them. If you *don't* behave in these ways, I shall doubt that you really do believe that fire burns – whatever you say.

This may also apply in religious belief. Perhaps the Sermon on the Mount is not so much a set of divine commands, which contrast strongly with our own natural concerns, as it is an account of 'the way in which anyone who genuinely and wholeheartedly believes in the heavenly Father' – as Jesus did – would 'naturally tend to live': believing 'that this is God's world and that we are in his hands' (Hick, 1983, p. 63). Believing has implications and consequences in behaviour.

TO DO

Read Matthew 6.19—7.5. Should we interpret these sayings as the natural *implications* of certain beliefs about God?

If we did, how would that affect how we think about – and how we teach others about – Christian ethics?

Faith: bigger believing

Most beliefs involve nothing more than believing that something is true (that Mercury lies nearer to the sun than the earth does; that John is late arriving home this evening). Such 'beliefs-that' or 'beliefs about' are components of religious believing as well, including the beliefs that God exists, that Christ died on a cross (a historical belief) and that he died for our sins (a theological belief). However, many beliefs about persons and causes – and about God, Christ and the Church, too – include some additional elements. Although people often treat the two phrases equally, *belief in* someone or something involves much more than *believing that* this person or thing (God, Christ, George, baptism, democracy) exists, or believing that some claim about them is true (see Romans 10.9; James 2.9). These extra features are:

- a positive evaluation: we are 'for' George, we are in favour of him, we approve of him; and we are 'for' God, we regard God as possessing supreme worth – and therefore offer God our worship ('worth-ship') (perhaps John 20.26–30 and Philippians 2.5–11 illustrate this element);
- an attitude of trust or reliance, and sometimes of hope (e.g. Acts 14.9; Hebrews 11);
- a commitment, expressed in acting out our positive attitudes towards a person, thing or ideal; in religion, this involves commitment and obedience to God (e.g. Luke 6.46–49; James 2.14–23; Revelation 2.13).

The word *faith* is often used to describe this sort of religious believing-in, in which case it is more than just intellectual assent. This brings in the affective (feeling) side of a person, and fits the definition of belief – offered by some psychologists – as 'an emotional acceptance'. This seems to be a good account of the nature of religious faith, which Calvin described as 'more of the heart than of the brain, and more of the disposition than of the understanding'. Many people believe that God exists who do not much care about

God and certainly don't go so far as worshipping or following God. But to believe *in* God, one might say, is to believe-that God *with attitude* (and with the corresponding commitment to action).

Unfortunately, Christians have from time to time disagreed over this definition, with Catholics treating faith as if it were identical to belief-that (and then adding that such assent must be assisted by God's grace and 'completed by love'), while Protestants tend to see true faith as already including personal commitment and active trust in God (while assuming that it also involves convictions about the existence and nature of God). When you read about the arguments during the Reformation over whether justification – that is, 'entering into the right relationship with God' – is or is not 'through faith alone', you may wish to recall this disagreement over the meaning of the word 'faith' (see Chapter 8, and Astley, 2010, pp. 116–20).

Another contrast worth noting in the theological context is that between the object (or content or 'deposit') of faith, and its subject (or process, experience and response): that is, between

- the faith that is believed (*the* Christian faith); and
- the faith through which it is believed (*our* Christian faith).

In a sense this is a theoretical contrast, because 'there is no faith without a content toward which it is directed' (Tillich, 1957, p. 10). Nevertheless, it captures a worthwhile distinction. 'To affirm Christian faith is to say I believe what the church believes. Simultaneously, it is to say these beliefs are mine, they go to the center of who I am, and refer to what I take to be most trustworthy about life' (Inbody, 2005, p. 3).

Is faith reasonable?

Many present-day theologians do not think that we can prove the existence of God by reason alone, that is without the aid of God's revelation and/or our religious experience. Some, however, still defend a natural theology (see Chapter 2) that seeks to prove God's existence as an explanation for the existence and 'design' of the universe, or even as a necessary implication of the idea of God.

At the other extreme, some religious thinkers are *fideists* (literally 'faith-ists'), claiming that we must rely on a faith that is wholly beyond and independent of reason. Tertullian (*c.* 160–225) is notorious for his rejection of (pagan) philosophy. 'What is there in common between Athens and Jerusalem?', he asked. (However, the phrase often attributed to him, 'I believe because it is absurd', is a misquotation.) The Danish philosopher Søren Kierkegaard (1813–55) argued that faith needs no rational justification. Reason can only get us so far. In order to embrace some of the key, paradoxical truths of Christianity one must make a personal decision through a leap of (or, better, 'to' and 'by') faith – a leap into the arms of the gracious God who gives us the gift of faith.

This is one way of making sense of faith as being both ours *and* God's. If faith is only appropriated by our response, then faith is 'both gift and choice. True faith is a gift that is freely accepted' (Tilley, 2010, p. 55).

Most theologians hold that our human faith, while it goes beyond reason, should never be *contrary to* reason and must therefore always be open to questioning, evidence and doubt. Faith goes beyond what is known (or 'seen' – cf. 2 Corinthians 5.7; Hebrews 11.1) and what can be proved, but not in a way that blindly ignores all the evidence or rational arguments brought against it.

If we think about this, it is not so odd. If you 'have faith' in a person – if, for example, you trust George's explanation why he has arrived so late, and his promise to come earlier tomorrow – you base your faith on evidence and reasoning, especially the evidence you have of George's character and behaviour, and your reasoning about them. But if you stumble across too much contrary evidence, or too many implausible excuses, you will – and perhaps you should? – 'lose faith' in him. Human faith, therefore, like religious faith,

> is never exactly a 'leap in the dark' … but a leap across to somewhere that isn't as brightly lit as the jumping-off point. Such 'going beyond' what is known is something that happens daily,

whenever we trust the promises of a friend or a lover, a train driver or airline pilot; or any 'authority' whose knowledge, skill and insight goes beyond our own. (Astley, 2010, p. 43)

Practice: what a performance!

People often say that they don't want to get involved with theology or belief, because they are practical folk. They only want 'a practical Christianity'. That's fair enough. In the end, is there any other sort of Christianity? If 'practice' is about action, application, doing things, *carrying on*, then Christianity is essentially a practice. Luke called Christianity the 'Way' (Acts 9.2; 19.9, 23; 24.22).

Some have developed the idea of Christian practice in faith terms, talking of 'faith as doing' or 'active faith' (cf. pp. 39–41 above). We often say that people's faith is 'in their doing'. This is a biblical insight, as the Bible's understanding of 'knowing' God involves acknowledging and worshipping God, and doing the will of God: it is a total, 'practical, intellectual and experiential matter' (Haymes, 1988, p. 120; cf. Exodus 5.2; Job 28.28; Jeremiah 22.16; Hosea 6.6; 8.1–3; John 6.29; 1 John 2.3–6).

These 'non-verbal' forms of faith are usually accompanied by words of faith, but not always. Nor are they always – or always just – moral actions. Ceremonies of worship and spiritual practices are also 'forms of faith'.

You may come across the Greek word *praxis*, chiefly in the context of a 'liberation theology' that focuses on people's freedom from oppression as the essence of their salvation. Praxis may sometimes simply be another word for 'practice', but usually it labels 'value-laden action' or reflective practice – 'action and reflection working together' (Graham, 1996, p. 7; Green, 2009, p. 7). Praxis has been described as 'the fundamental locus of theology, the "place" where theology occurs' (Boff, 2009, p. xxi).

Those who place practice (or praxis) at the centre of Christianity frequently understand it very broadly, as something that covers but is not restricted to our outer behaviour. Thus Thomas Groome adopts a holistic ('whole person') perspective, arguing that life is simply 'what we are doing, thinking and feeling', and includes our relationships and experiences as well as our lived responses and actions. 'Concern for the practical', on this account, is concern 'for everyday living' in all its fullness (Groome, 2011, pp. 275–6).

Within practical theology (see Chapter 6), theology is a discipline whose task it is to describe how a particular practice, situation or life is a *theology-in-practice* (Graham, 1996, p. 7). In this case, practice is understood to have its own theological authority as the bearer of 'embodied theology' (Cameron et al., 2010, p. 51). It is frequently seen as the *performance*, or acting out, of the 'text' of an individual's or group's beliefs, values, theories and theologies that underpin it (Swinton and Mowat, 2006, pp. 19–20).

Further reading

Astley, J., 2007, *Christ of the Everyday*, London: SPCK, especially Chs 1, 2 and 8.

Green, L., 2009, *Let's Do Theology: Resources for Contextual Theology*, London: Mowbray.

Groome, T. H., 2011, *Will There Be Faith? Depends on Every Christian*, Dublin: Veritas, Chs 3 and 4.

Hauerwas, S. with Goldstone, B., 2011, 'Disciplined Seeing: Forms of Christianity and Forms of Life', in Stanley Hauerwas, *Learning to Speak Christian*, London: SCM Press, pp. 33–60.

Williams, R., 2007, *Tokens of Trust: An Introduction to Christian Belief*, Norwich: Canterbury Press, Ch. 1.

5

Theology's Main Sources: Bible and Tradition

Our theology comes from somewhere. Some of it, inevitably, comes from ourselves. We have a theological voice of our own. This must always be the case to some extent – as I argued in Chapters 1 and 2 – because for any theology to be *our* theology we must embrace and own it, and even make our own original contribution to it and individual critique of it. We are always, in part, working out our own theology, if only by using our reason to reflect on and assess the theology we receive from others, and developing that theology into something that is of significance to our own needs, context and concerns.

Nevertheless, much Christian theology is *learned*, including the concepts and criteria that we use to reflect on and evaluate our own theology and that of other people. And Christians have traditionally learned their theology from two great teachers in particular: the Bible, and the traditions and experience of the Church.

Using the Bible

The Bible is often viewed as a sign of the unity of the Church (which, as we noted in Chapter 2, is a unity-with-diversity, like the human body – cf. Romans 7.4; 1 Corinthians 12.12–30). Sadly, however, the Bible can lead to disagreement and division as well.

It sometimes seems that the only thing about the Bible on which everyone agrees is its list of contents, the 'canon'. Alas, the effect of human hands is only too visible even there. For different Christian groups disagree on the status of the 'Apocrypha': that is, books such as Ecclesiasticus, Esther and Tobit, which were written in Greek rather than Hebrew. Roman Catholics integrate them throughout their Old Testament (as in *The Jerusalem Bible*), whereas Anglicans and others often gather them together in a separate section between the two Testaments, as books read 'for example of life and instruction in manners ... [not] to establish any doctrine' (*Thirty-Nine Articles of Religion*, 1562, Art. VI). Many other Protestant Churches omit these texts altogether.[1]

But even where there is agreement over content, there are widely divergent views about how the Bible should be interpreted and employed. Many Protestants or 'Evangelicals' call themselves 'Bible-believing' Christians, implying that they assign all authority over Christian belief and practice to this book – or, rather, these books, for the Bible is made up of a great diversity of different texts. Some are *fundamentalists*, claiming that – as the Bible contains no errors at all – it can serve as an authoritative guide not only in its teaching about doctrine and ethics, but also in its history and science. Clearly they represent a group of biblical 'conservatives', but many who adopt that description for themselves are not fundamentalists. *Conservatives* simply seek to preserve or return to traditional beliefs: in this case, basing their own faith largely on the Bible's account of the history of salvation, its morality, its broad theological themes and ideas, or even just its imagery. For conservatives these things are seen as authoritative givens, which human reflection and critique can never overthrow. Even here there is diversity, however, for such conservatives may be either Protestant or Catholic. The former, as we have seen, tend to bestow authority solely on biblical events or themes; while the latter group give a similar, if not quite equal, authority to the teachings and practices of the continuing Church (that is, 'Church tradition').

Liberal is a title claimed by many Christians, within many denominations, who think of themselves as being more free (the Latin word

---

1 The practice of praying for the dead, encouraged by the apocryphal books of Maccabees but not elsewhere in Scripture, is said to express the sole doctrinal difference between Protestants and Catholics that depends on the different value each group places on these books.

liber means 'free') to interpret Scripture and tradition from their own perspective, by using their own reason and contemporary experience. They are more likely than conservatives to claim that biblical ideas are 'of their own time', and need to be *reinterpreted* in order to serve as God's word for us today. In engaging in such reinterpretation, liberals do not think that they are denying that Scripture has a unique authority. But they insist that when its words are communicated to us today they should be treated as one partner within a two-way conversation, in which the other partner – the Christian's own independent voice, equipped with today's knowledge and ideas – cannot be silenced. Liberals consistently oppose fundamentalism, arguing that God's revelation always comes through fallible human intermediaries whose 'hearing' and recording of God's word is not immunized from human error. According to my dictionary, liberal theologians regard 'many traditional beliefs as dispensable, invalidated by modern thought, or liable to change' (*Concise Oxford English Dictionary*, eleventh edition). Note the 'or' in this definition, which suggests that some liberals are much less radical than others.

It is true, of course, that 'conservative' and 'liberal' are rather vague terms that differ in degree rather than in kind. We should picture a continuous spectrum of views with 'extreme conservatives' and 'extreme liberals' positioned at the two ends, and a range of rather indefinite positions located between them. In recent years, both ends of this spectrum have themselves fragmented into a range of different positions.

TO DO

Where would you locate yourself among these different ways of viewing the accuracy of the Bible? (Perhaps answering the questionnaire below, by ticking the box that best represents your response to its statements, might help you to be clearer about your true position.[2])

---

2 For the responses of others to these and similar questions, see Astley and Day, 1992, ch. 25; Astley, 2000, ch. 8; Francis, Robbins and Astley, 2005.

Is the Bible accurate?

	Agree strongly	Agree	Not certain	Disagree	Disagree strongly
The Bible is always accurate when it describes history					
The Bible is always accurate when it talks about scientific matters					
The Bible is always accurate when it talks about God, God's acts and God's will for humans					
The Bible is always accurate when it talks about how people should behave					

Diversity and the Bible

The way in which people use the Bible is going to have a profound effect on how they formulate and defend Christian teaching. Many would say that theology and ethics must be entirely dependent on the Bible, as there can be no other authoritative source for what we should believe and how we should behave. We should, however, note two facts that this standpoint appears to overlook:

1 Bible-believing Christians often disagree among themselves about what Christians should believe and do;
2 the Bible itself contains a diversity of teaching and moral exhortation, which sometimes appears to conflict.

TO DO

Look up the following pairs of biblical passages. How would you respond to the apparent contradictions between them?

1 Samuel 17.1–11, 48–51	cf.	2 Samuel 21.18–22
2 Samuel 24.24	cf.	1 Chronicles 21.25
John 20.28	cf.	Mark 10.17–18

It would appear from such accounts (which differ, admittedly, on fairly trivial issues) that it is impossible to hold that the Bible is infallible: that is, incapable of ever being wrong. However you respond to this sort of diversity within Scripture, it is hard to deny that diversity is present there.

At a deeper level, there also appears to be a fair amount of *theological* diversity within the Christian Scriptures. For example, the Bible does not appear to speak 'with a single voice' across the following themes:

- the importance of ritual worship   Exodus chs 29 and 30   cf. Hosea 6.6; Amos 5.21–25

- the explanation of human suffering   Psalm 37.25   cf. Ecclesiastes 9.11; Luke 13.4–5

- life after death   Psalm 6.5 and Psalm 88   cf. Psalm 139.8; Mark 12.24–27

- Jesus' knowledge   Matthew 11.27; John 16.30; 21.17   cf. Mark 5.30; 13.32

What should we make of these differences? Not all of them can be put down to 'progressive revelation' (see Chapter 2), not even when the differences fall between the Old and New Testaments. It is clear that there are diverse theologies within each. The New Testament scholar, James Dunn, writes:

> We can no longer doubt that there are *many different expressions of Christianity within* the NT [New Testament] ... The same faith in Jesus man and exalted one had to come to expression in words in a variety of different individuals and circumstances ... When we ask about the Christianity of the NT we are not asking about any one entity, rather we encounter different types of Christianity ... [and each of these] was itself not monochrome and homogenous, rather more like a spectrum. (Dunn, 1977, pp. 372–4)

> The unity of the NT can be conceived and grasped only as a unity in diversity, that is, a unity that is like the unity of the body, a single identity composed of and made possible by the integration and interaction of the diverse parts. (Dunn, 2009, p. 8)

The response of many theologians to such matters is to claim that 'what the Bible supplies us with is the raw material for doctrine, not the finished product itself'. This allows them to claim that the Bible is to be seen as 'evidence, witness, testimony' to God, not as a manual or prescriptive handbook for theology or ethics (Hanson and Hanson, 1981, pp. 46–7).

Interpretation and inspiration

It should also be recognized that the way we read and interpret the Bible does not wholly derive from the Bible itself. How could it?

Look up 2 Timothy 3.16–17 and 2 Peter 1.20–21 (and also, if you can access it, a more explicit text from the Apocrypha, 2 Esdras 14.37–48). In order to interpret passages such as these as supporting a fundamentalist view of Scripture, you must already be convinced (a) that their authors (or first readers?) themselves understood them in this way, which is a view that many biblical scholars reject, and (b) that they were correct in what they were claiming. Furthermore, there are books other than the Bible that contain within their pages claims to authority – sometimes even inerrancy – and most Christians would not accept those books 'as Scripture' (see Chapter 2).

It seems, rather, that fundamentalists *come to* the Bible wearing a particular set of interpretative spectacles. They have usually been taught to wear these aids to their biblical vision by the Churches to which they belong, which have passed on a particular tradition of biblical interpretation. (And, yes, the same may be said of all of us, including those who belong to more liberal Church traditions.)

In any case, there is so much in the Bible. At the very least, people want to know what are the *key* passages, beliefs or commands in Scripture, and which ones are less important. Many Christians are quite keen to sing the beautiful first six verses of Psalm 137 ('By the waters of Babylon – there we sat down and there we wept ...'). But far fewer go on to loudly endorse the views expressed in verse 8, in which the psalmist rejoices in the prospect of children belonging to Israel's enemy being dashed against a rock. (The same principle applies to the British National Anthem, whose additional verse – which hopes that Marshall Wade will crush the 'Rebellious Scots' – wasn't sung for long!)

So, however conservative or 'Bible-based' we believe ourselves to be, we are – all of us – always involved in selecting and prioritizing certain scriptural texts and books over other parts of the Bible, thereby constructing our own 'canon within the canon'. In doing so, we are making a judgement about the relative importance of these different parts. This interpretation, too, is something we largely bring to Scripture; it is only in part derived *from* Scripture. 'No one depends on a simple reading of the Bible for faith or practice. Everyone approaches the Bible with a theology in hand' (Inbody, 2005, p. 8). *Everyone.*

This is not to be condemned. It is inevitable, and mostly a good thing. I suspect that as many people are put off religion as are converted to it, by reading the Bible without the assistance of more experienced interpreters and their explicit or implicit theologies. The Bible begins with Genesis, and untutored readers who begin there and continue from book to book will quickly find themselves deep into the ritual laws of Leviticus (e.g. chapters 4 or 15). To ask if this is the best place to begin is to ask a question that the Bible itself doesn't really answer. But Churches ought to have an answer to it, and we should grant that such practical questions about how the Bible should be read require a *theological* answer about what the Bible is really about, and how it is best interpreted.

One of the key theological issues at stake here is what we mean by the 'inspiration' of Scripture. The term seems to suggest that God is *in some sense* the 'author' of Scripture, and thus that those who wrote these texts were prompted and moved, influenced and directed, perhaps even wholly controlled by God's Spirit. Yet it appears to be impossible to hold that every statement of the Bible is true in every respect – that is, inerrant (see above, pp. 46–8), which would surely be the case if the writers of Scripture were like pens in the hand of the divine author – as the sixth-century Pope Gregory put it, along with today's advocates of 'plenary' inspiration.

But three centuries before Gregory, Origen had argued that the outer form of Scripture bears the mark of its human authors (and not always in a positive way), although he thought that this left the inner truth untouched. It was this, more liberal, view that eventually developed into a doctrine of inspiration in which divine truth was viewed as contained and communicated in Scripture, as elsewhere, through earthen vessels (or 'clay jars', in more recent translations of 2 Corinthians 4.7). On this view, 'God speaks to us in a manner congruous with the Incarnation itself [the 'enfleshing' of God in Christ], through human words and human minds conditioned by the circumstances of place and time, subject to our ordinary limitations.' These human minds may have been inspired so as to 'discern the true spiritual significance of history', for example, 'but they are none the less liable to error and ignorance' (Lampe, 1963, p. 142). This is no mechanical, inerrant inspiration. Some argue that biblical inspiration is something much more continuous with the inspiration we might claim for the work of a contemporary novelist, poet, painter, philosopher or even scientist. It involves God's 'guidance' or 'revelation', but not in a way that is infallible and therefore immune from criticism – at least not when its recipients think about it and commit it to (their own) writing (see Chapter 2).

Should we be concerned about the possibility of error in Scripture? Not according to those who welcome this more human view of inspiration for theological reasons.

If we are embarrassed by the humanity of the biblical writers, we are also probably embarrassed by the humanity of Jesus the Jew from Nazareth and by our own humanity ... If we affirm the full humanity of Jesus, we will also respect the humanity of the biblical witnesses. (Migliore, 2004, p. 54).

As Christians we ought to desire to live under the authority of God, and under the authority of persons or things only as they minister to us the authority of God ... The desire for an infallibility short of the infallibility of God, be it of Church or Bible, is an idolatrous lust. (Evans, 1960, p. 32)

TO DO

How do you react to the above claims by a systematic theologian (Migliore) and New Testament scholar (Evans)?

Would it matter to your view of the authority of Scripture if you were to be persuaded that neither the Bible nor the Church's teaching is infallible?[3] If so, why? If not, why not?

Bible versus tradition?

The way you responded to the earlier parts of this chapter is also likely to reveal where you stand in the battle over Christian *tradition*. Radical Protestants have claimed that, as Scripture alone contains all that is necessary for Christian salvation, nothing – and certainly nothing contributed by the Church – should ever be added to it, for 'adding of this kind always results in subtracting. This should be clear once we see that the Bible is not only supreme but *sufficient*. Add to what is complete and you take away from it' (Wallis, 1981, p. 109).

---

3 The infallibility of some papal or Church definitions of 'faith or morals' is supported by Roman Catholic theology, under certain restricted circumstances.

This was not the view of the classic leaders of Protestantism in the sixteenth-century Reformation, however, despite their watchword *sola scriptura* ('by Scripture alone'). Luther, Calvin and their followers, and the theologians who influenced the English Reformation, all held to a doctrine of the supremacy of Scripture. Yet they all also took over the creeds, most of the doctrines and at least some aspects of the worship and other practices of the Church that they sought to reform, and from which they eventually separated; retaining whatever did not conflict with their gospel of justification by grace through faith. According to Arthur Wallis, 'This non-radical attitude of the reformers left many unscriptural traditions untouched [and] needing to be challenged' (Wallis, 1981, p. 110). But for the great majority of Protestants, tradition is thought of as something that completes, enhances or improves the revelation contained in and conveyed by Scripture. Most Roman Catholic and Eastern Orthodox theologians take a similar or even stronger view.

Historically, the importance of an authoritative tradition that tells Christians how they should interpret their sacred Scripture became obvious when, in the second century, heretics such as the Gnostics arose claiming to have a secret knowledge that was key to securing salvation, and interpreted the Bible to fit in with their ideas. Early champions of Christian orthodoxy, such as Irenaeus (*c*. 130–*c*. 200), argued that the 'apostolic tradition' handed down from the apostles by their successors the bishops showed the Church how to understand these texts in the correct (apostolic) manner. 'Tradition is thus the guarantor of faithfulness to the original apostolic teaching, a safeguard against the innovations and misrepresentations of biblical texts' (McGrath, 2008, p. xxii).

A 'tradition' is simply something that is passed on (from the Latin for 'give' plus 'across'), and has always been – and still is – 'a living process … of subtracting and adding, appropriating and reshaping of the past' (Inbody, 2005, p. 41). Much of the Bible itself began as stories and teaching that were passed on, and passed down through the generations, well before any of it was committed to paper. This is as true of the stories about Jesus and his teaching as it is of the tales about the tribes of Israel and their beliefs (see 1 Corinthians

15.1–7). For tens of years in the first case, and hundreds in the second, these elements were passed on by word of mouth – as an 'oral tradition'. This later became a 'written tradition' of documents that were copied, and sometimes miscopied and even sometimes deliberately amended, until they resulted in the Greek and Hebrew manuscripts that form the basis of our present English translations (or 'versions'). What we read in our Bibles is thus already the result of a long process of 'handing on' – that is, of tradition. On this account, therefore, tradition *precedes* Scripture as we now have it. And many claim that tradition not only has but *must* always accompany Scripture, as it is tradition that tells us how to read and use the biblical texts.

Is revelation over?

When thinking about revelation in Chapter 2, we mainly focused on the Bible. However, the Church's tradition, which is always facing new issues and different cultural situations and assumptions, may be thought of as a *continuing revelation* that can provide new and deeper insights into, and understandings and applications of, the original revelation.

> In this continuing or dependent revelation we meet God in Christ through the Spirit just as really and truly as did the apostles, but this meeting is mediated to us by the testimony of the apostles recorded in the Bible and commented on, proclaimed, taught, and re-enacted by the church. (Thomas, 1983, p. 34)

As you would expect, some even argue that later tradition may also, on occasions, critique the original scriptural revelation, correcting and adding to it and not just clarifying it. In this case, tradition and Scripture may be said to be in a more equal dialogue or conversation with each other, 'with now one yielding, now the other'. This might suggest that God is 'constantly responding to changed circumstances rather than implanting hidden meanings [in Scripture] that are only subsequently brought to light' (Brown, 1999, pp. 111, 131). New revelations therefore arise as and when individuals at a particular point in time are 'inspired to propose that meaning' (Brown, 1994, p. 40). On such a view, God's inspiration and revelation continues beyond Scripture.

Christians will disagree about the most likely or significant locations for such continuing revelations. Protestantism tends to be more open to claims by individuals, in particular within charismatic and Pentecostal traditions, while insisting on 'testing the spirits' – particularly against the measure of the canonical Scriptures (see Chapter 2). Roman Catholics have tended to view their bishops as having their own teaching authority, distinct from – though closely related to – Scripture. This is the *magisterium* of the Church, a living tradition that involves contemporary reflection on theological truths in response to the changed circumstances of today's world. The Eastern Orthodox Churches hold a similar view of a 'living tradition'.

Practising tradition

But we should not think of tradition simply in terms of revelation or scriptural interpretation. The idea of Christian tradition can be very wide. According to the Catholic theologian Terrence Tilley:

> A religious tradition is best understood as an enduring practice or set of practices including a vision (belief), attitudes (disposition, affections), and patterns of action ... Knowing a tradition is much more fundamentally a knowing *how* to live in and live out a tradition ... Traditions are best understood as communicative practices, in which the communication of the 'how to' is as important as, or more important than, much of the 'what' communicated. How to love God with one's whole mind, whole heart, and whole self is primary; doctrines about God, mind, heart and self are derivative. (Tilley, 2000, pp. 45, 80)

TO DO

How do you respond to Tilley's account of tradition?

Try to list the different elements in the Church's life, other than the Bible, that embody and pass on these ways of believing, valuing, belonging, acting and experiencing. How are all these Christian practices passed on?

Can Tilley's account be applied to the Bible as well? May we think of the Bible as part of a wider notion of 'Christian tradition', and as one of the main things that Christians pass on – and that also 'works' by showing us how to love God?

Further reading

Astley, J., 2010, *SCM Studyguide to Christian Doctrine*, London: SCM Press, pp. 29–39.

Barr, J., 1984, *Escaping from Fundamentalism*, London: SCM Press.

Hodgson, P. C., 1994, *Winds of the Spirit: A Constructive Christian Theology*, London: SCM Press, Ch. 2.

Inbody, T., 2005, *The Faith of the Christian Church: An Introduction to Theology*, Grand Rapids, MI: Eerdmans, Ch. 2.

McGrath, A. E., 2007, *Christian Theology: An Introduction*, Oxford: Blackwell, Ch. 6.

Migliore, D. L., 2004, *Faith Seeking Understanding: An Introduction to Christian Theology*, Grand Rapids, MI: Eerdmans, Ch. 3.

Morgan, R. with Barton, J., 1988, *Biblical Interpretation*, Oxford: Oxford University Press.

Strange, W., 2000, *The Authority of the Bible*, London: Darton, Longman & Todd.

6

Theological Subjects, Skills and Methods

In this chapter we shall look at the different disciplines and skills that are used in the broad field of Christian theological study, together with the subject areas to which they relate.

Much of the material in this book concentrates on theology in terms of our talk of God which expresses and explores Christian beliefs about God – and, by extension, about Christ, the Spirit, creation, salvation, the Church, heaven, and so on. This usage tends to equate theology with a particular *discipline* – that is to say, a way of knowing and thinking – largely, in this case, systematic or philosophical theology (see below).

As we saw in Chapter 3, however, the word 'theology' is not just used for the *beliefs* people hold, or the processes of thinking that change these beliefs (of which theology as belief is a 'product'). It is a term that also applies to the *study of these beliefs*. When 'Christian theology' is used to label studies of this field or area (of Christian believing), it often draws on a wider range of different disciplines or ways of knowing, understanding and critiquing Christian beliefs. These specialities raise particular issues for the theology that we may hold as individuals, and that of the Church as a whole.

We shall now review the main examples of these theological disciplines, mentioning some of the concerns that they address.

Biblical studies

Many ordinary Christians, and some textbooks and courses, assume that the Bible is the only source book of Christian beliefs and its study should be all that is required in studying theology. In Chapters 2 and 5, I offered some thoughts about the place of Scripture in the mix of sources for Christian theology. While the study of the Bible is fundamental to our tasks of understanding and doing theology, understanding the Bible is not identical to these tasks. This is partly because the Bible itself contains a variety of theologies or ways of thinking about God, and partly because how the Bible impacts on our theology will depend on how we view and interpret it. We can never get away from *our* role as active interpreters of the biblical – or of all other – texts. This is one of the major problems faced by biblical scholars.

Many new students are surprised, and sometimes horrified, by the way that academics treat the Bible. Since at least the eighteenth century, scholars have engaged in what is usually described as *biblical criticism*: 'that approach to the study of Scripture which consciously searches for and applies the canons of reason to its investigation of the text', using 'canon' here in the sense of a rule by which something is judged (Soulen, 1977, p. 26). Of course, this view assumes that the Bible is accessible to human reasoning, and in particular to our historical reasoning, treating it (in words that make many Christians uneasy) 'like any other book'.[1]

However, biblical scholars have increasingly recognized that many parts of the books of the Old and New Testaments are themselves theological texts with religious content, and not just historical sources 'like any other'. Thus the New Testament writings constitute 'specific ways of interpreting [the] new religious convictions and experiences' of the first-century communities and individuals that lie behind them (Johnson, 2010, p. 14). In so far as our own individual theology, and the Church's theology in general, wishes to take seriously its biblical roots and the primordial revelation to

---

1 This is Benjamin Jowett's notorious phrase, from his essay in the 1860 collection, *Essays and Reviews* (p. 338).

which the Bible bears witness, we must share in that continuing task of theological interpretation, for our time and in our own context. Further, as the Bible is first and foremost the book of and for a religion, it must still be possible 'to read the Bible religiously (on the assumption that it speaks of God)': that is, to read the Bible *as Scripture* (Morgan with Barton, 1988, pp. 36, 38).

Again, our own responsibility as theologians and interpreters of theology remains a key consideration. It is not honest to list 'proof-texts' from Scripture for particular doctrinal positions, unless we are also willing to search out and to cite other, apparently equally 'authoritative' texts that appear to support a different view. Such different theologies are readily available to anyone who takes the trouble to study the whole Bible, and who refuses to focus solely on the limited 'canon within the canon' that reflects one particular theology.

If we are to use the Bible more seriously, we are going to have to do some work ourselves. A great deal of this will involve relating our contemporary theology to the Bible. This 'relating' is never just a one-way process. As you will recall, it is a dialogue or conversation in which theological thinking helps us to interpret and critique Scripture, as well as Scripture providing the potent language, narratives and insights that serve as the raw material for developing (and criticizing) our theology. A naive model of 'applying the Bible' to contemporary concerns is not really helpful here. As the Old Testament scholar, James Barr, has written:

> As for involvement in what are called 'the burning issues of the day', biblical studies are of course a factor in the mind of the religious communities. But the Bible does not, in most cases, give in itself a decision on such matters ... More is to be said in favour of the view ... that we begin with the present day and then consider the Bible, not alone, but as part of the mixture of relevant factors, including the traditions which historically connect us back to the Bible. (Barr, 1999, p. 607)

There is no doubt that this advice applies to many current ethical dilemmas and questions about the Church's practice, but it surely also applies to the Christian's thinking about what are the burning issues for her or his own theology.

We must also bear in mind a central claim of hermeneutics: the meaning of a text is not exhausted by what its author intended to say, which in any case may no longer be discoverable to readers who live in an age well beyond its original context (and may be quite unintelligible to them). The meaning a text has *for us*, as theologians thinking in our own time and culture, only really arises in our interaction today with this text from thousands of years ago.

These comments relate primarily to the *meaning* of biblical texts. People are also concerned about their *truth*. They ask, 'Is the Bible reliable?' In reply, one can at least say this. The historical context of the Bible has been critically studied by very many researchers – in the company of a great industry of other scholarly disciplines, skills and insights – more intensely than any other book (or collection of books). If we can make any reliable historical claims about the world of thousands of years ago, it will be in this area of study. But note that even a wholly convincing defence of the 'historicity' of biblical events and characters cannot serve as a defence of the theological beliefs that these people held, or which these events are said to express. And that is because theological truth and divine revelation do not appear in history in the same sort of verifiable way as do events such as the exodus or the crucifixion. This is unambiguously shown by the fact that different people can agree in believing that these events happened, yet radically disagree about their theological meaning – and even as to whether they can have such a meaning at all.

Christian theology may be *based on* Christian history, but there is no knock-down logical argument that forces us to move from one to the other.

TO DO

Reflect on the part that a critical study of the Bible is likely to play in your own theology.

Systematic and philosophical theology

These twin disciplines represent attempts, sometimes at a highly abstract and intellectually demanding level, to create:

- either an account of the whole body of Christian beliefs organized into an orderly system that is coherent, connected and consistent, and is tested against the norms of Scripture and tradition (see Chapter 6) (as 'systematic' or 'dogmatic' theology);
- or an analysis, clarification and (sometimes) defence of theological concepts and arguments, using the tools and insights of philosophy (as 'philosophical' theology).

These academic approaches together contribute to and comprise the particular 'discipline' of theology that we discussed at the beginning of this chapter: that is, theology understood as reflective Christian belief, rather than as a range of separate disciplines that explore (different parts or sources of) Christian belief from different angles, wielding the different tools of the biblical scholar, the historian, and so on.

> **TO DO**
>
> Look back at what was said in Chapters 1–3 about academic theology. How important is it to you that your own beliefs should be open to the tests and criticisms of reason, Scripture and tradition, and the insights of academic theology?

Historical theology

I have often heard students, or their Christian pastors and friends, scolding those who teach biblical studies or systematic and philosophical theology as enemies of Christianity who create in the minds of students doubts and uncertainties that tend to undermine their faith. But my own experience has been that the most corrosive of theology's academic sub-disciplines is actually church history, particularly 'historical theology'.

This has been defined as 'the branch of theology which aims to explore the historical situations within which ideas developed or were specifically formulated', and 'to lay bare the connections between context and theology' (McGrath, 2007, p. 108). According to Alister McGrath, studies like this provide the strongest evidence that 'there is a *provisional* or *conditional* element to Christian theology' that makes it rather independent of its fundamental resources. This is a key challenge of the history of Christian thought.

Theology has developed down the ages – its ideas and emphases have come and changed, and often gone. In some cases, what was seen by the Church to be true and important in one age was rejected by the Church in another. Theology has a history – as does my theology, and yours. I think that we need to be more honest (and more humble) about this. This is not to say that 'Relativism Rules OK' but only that human beings are human and that they don't always get things right. (Not at first, anyway; but sometimes not at the tenth time, either.)

But here is a more positive account of the role of historical theology:

Historical theology ... fills the gap between the time of God's Word and the present time of the church's word by studying the church's word in the intervening periods. In so doing it has a triple function. First, it shows how the church and its word, moving across the centuries and continents, have come from there to here with an ongoing continuity in spite of every discontinuity. Second, it offers examples of the way in which, and the reasons why, the conformity of the church's word to God's Word has been achieved or compromised in the different centuries and settings. Third, it brings to the church of today a valuable accumulation of enduring insights as well as relevant hints and warnings. It plays, then, a substantive, if for the most part auxiliary, role which dogmatic and pastoral theology will quickly accept if they are about their proper business. (Bromiley, 1978, p. xxvi)

We may consider a further point here. Biblical scholars and philosophers may sometimes seem to be hypercritical of some of our own favourite elements within the Christian faith. We are often worried by such excessive criticism. But the historian is even more likely to come to his texts with an attitude of 'suspicion and distrust', for this is part and parcel of being a historian, too.

> He must not accept the evidence of his sources at their face value without first submitting them to critical scrutiny. Most of the documents available to him were written not to provide the future historian with a balanced selection of evidence but to make out a particular case. (Wiles, 1976, p. 35)

But don't we *want* the historical foundations of our theology to be subjected to such rigorous testing? (And if not, why not?)

TO DO

How do you assess the positive and negative contributions of historical theology?

What examples would you cite?

Practical theology

As we have stressed more than once, Christianity is not just a set of beliefs. It is mainly a matter of living, of engaging in 'Christian practices' – which include care and compassion, prayer and worship, evangelism and teaching, and social and political action. These are not to be thought of as *applications* of theology – as if Christian beliefs, virtues, attitudes and insights were first worked out in some pure, rarefied manner and then *applied* to a world with which they haven't so far been involved. Christian practices are, rather, essential aspects of a whole-person, lived Christianity that incorporates practice along with beliefs (theology) and Christian feelings and emotions (see Chapter 4). Christian theology, on one understanding, is itself an 'ecclesial practice', one of the many activities of the Church (Stiver, 2009, p. 3).

Practical theology is essentially 'the study of the norms and principles of the practice of the church and its members' (Thomas, 1983, p. 13). Christian reflection on Christian practice always has an underlying theological dimension. This is not something alien that is imposed on independent practice, but comprises a framework of Christian meanings and values that come to expression in such Christian activity. In colleges, courses, seminaries and universities, syllabuses of 'practical theology' make this link explicit in their *theologies of* worship, Christian education, evangelism, preaching, social and liberating action, and – particularly – pastoral care (hence 'pastoral theology').

In a sense, *all* Christian theology is practical theology if all theology ultimately arises in a dialogue between Christians and their lives and experiences, and the Christian sources or traditions. Most exponents of practical theology see its component of theological reflection as arising out of the exploration of our human engagement and action, and the experiences that run along with them; with our response to this reflection eventually informing our Christian practice again, in an ever-revolving 'pastoral cycle', 'learning cycle' or 'doing theology spiral' (see Green, 2009, ch. 2).

TO DO

Look back at the discussion of practice in Chapter 4, and the suggestions of a 'holistic view' that sees practice, alongside belief and experience, as one dimension of a single, multi-dimensional person. This account suggests that practice is usually accompanied by and expressed in beliefs. But are there also some religious beliefs that are not expressed in any practice, or any religious practices that imply no particular theological beliefs?

Skills and methods in theology

General study skills

It is worth remarking that the academic study of theology requires a range of skills of reading, study, writing and discussion that are broadly similar to those required by other 'arts' or 'humanities' students (see Ackroyd and Major, 1999). Theology may be unique with respect to its subject matter, but much of it is studied 'like any other subject'.

Language skills

Theology is a study that mainly involves studying texts, from the Bible and other theologians throughout history. Unfortunately, not all of these are in English. I once witnessed a discussion between a theological college staff member who taught the Old Testament and a mature student who had just discovered that this tutor could not read Hebrew. 'How can you teach the Old Testament without knowing Hebrew?' was his embarrassing question. 'Because there are so many excellent English translations available,' was the rather tetchy reply.

Learning Hebrew (and Greek for the New Testament) allows students access to 'a whole linguistic and cultural world' and 'a vast treasury of Jewish scriptural interpretations'; it also enables them to get behind the translations and interpretations, 'to engage with them afresh' and make their own judgements by appealing to the original text (Ford, 2013, pp. 132–3). On the other hand, learning languages is very time-consuming and requires specific aptitudes that not every student or every theologian will possess. Reading the Bible in its original language is the ideal, perhaps; but as long as biblical scholars continue translating and writing commentaries using the original texts, the rest of us can still 'enter into their labours' – in my case, with a sense of great relief.

Hermeneutical skills

David Ford offers us ten helpful guidelines for interpreting the meaning of texts, including religious texts (2013, pp. 137–9). They are not all possible in a given situation, but they provide a useful checklist at the back of the mind when confronted by any work of theology – whether a biblical text, a piece by a classical theologian or the work of a present-day writer. I summarize Ford's list below:

1 Ask about the *interrelation* of elements within the text, and with literature of its day and later.
2 Ask about its *genre* (parable, history, prayer, law, etc.).
3 Ask about the *author* and what the author intended to say.
4 Ask about the text's *context* (cultural, historical, etc.).
5 Ask about *other interpretations* of the text, between then and now.
6 Ask about *yourself*: your theological assumptions, presuppositions and 'interest' in the text. Why does it engage you?
7 Ask about its *theological truth*, as well as its meaning.
8 Be *suspicious* of the text and its interpretations (including your own), aware of the dangers of distortion, deception and oppression within any tradition.
9 Ask about the text's *relevance* and power, its 'imaginative and practical implications' (p. 138).
10 Recognize your need of a *community* of trusted interpretation.

TO DO

Are you happy to endorse all the items in Ford's checklist?

Which of these guidelines are the more significant ones for you?

Further reading

Ackroyd, R. and Major, D., 1999, *Shaping the Tools: Study Skills in Theology*, London: Darton, Longman & Todd.

Ballard, P. and Pritchard, J., 2006, *Practical Theology in Action: Christian Thinking in the Service of Church and Society*, London: SPCK.

Evans, R., 1999, *Using the Bible: Studying the Text*, London: Darton, Longman & Todd.

Ford, D., 2013, *Theology: A Very Short Introduction*, Oxford: Oxford University Press, Ch. 8.

McGrath, A. E., 2007, *Christian Theology: An Introduction*, Oxford: Blackwell, Ch. 5.

West, M., Noble, G. and Todd, A., 1999, *Living Theology*, London: Darton, Longman & Todd.

Wiles, M., 1976, *What is Theology?*, Oxford: Oxford University Press, Ch. II.

7

Human Language and the Mystery of God

According to the nineteenth-century French novelist Gustav Flaubert, our language is often wholly inadequate for our needs. He writes in *Madame Bovary*, 'Human speech is like a cracked kettle on which we tap crude tunes for bears to dance to, while we long to make music that will melt the stars.' Sadly, but inevitably, this is nowhere more obvious than in our religious or theological language.

We almost always learn our own language, as we learn much else, when we are very young – 'at our mother's knee' – and usually by just 'picking it up', rather than being explicitly taught its grammar and vocabulary. It is, fairly obviously, a *human* language. It is used to refer to and describe human beings and their actions ('pretty Mummy', 'naughty Daddy', 'fat Grandad') and other things that we can see, hear and touch. In other words, it is used of things in the world, which exist in our space and time.

This is the same language that we use to speak of and to God. But God is not 'a thing in the world'. God is the creator, the ultimate origin and continuous preserver, of the universe and everything in it. God exists independently of the universe, whereas the universe only exists in dependence on God's will. So between the creator and the created there is, inevitably, a great difference. The Protestant theologian Karl Barth, following Kierkegaard, called this the 'infinite qualitative distinction' between God and human beings, and made it one of the pivotal elements of his theology.

This difference between the creator and the creation is underlined by the fact that God exists 'outside' our space. God and heaven are not just 'above the bright blue sky', to quote the language of one Victorian hymn, not even in deep space: they are in another dimension altogether. God may act, and certainly God may be known, anywhere (literally any 'where'); and in that sense we may say that God is present everywhere ('omnipresent'). But that doesn't mean that you can catch God under your upturned glass, as you can a wasp. Nor can you locate God's position on any map, or tap in God's destination on any satnav. And you can't measure God's height or girth, either.

Christians also say that God has always existed and has no date of birth (and therefore no age), or any anticipated time of death. Many theologians believe that this is because God exists everlastingly: probably in a dimension of 'heavenly' time, which is no part of our temporal sequence although it can presumably interact with it. Such a God might be said to be 'in God's own time', so that 'a thousand years in your sight are like yesterday when it is past, or like a watch in the night' (Psalm 90.4). Others go even further, however, claiming that God is 'eternal' not just in the sense that God has no beginning or end, has always existed and shall always exist, but because God is 'outside all time' – truly time*less*. It is hard enough to imagine another temporal dimension for God, but we certainly don't have the imagery or the language adequately to describe a timeless God. In what sense could such a God 'act' or even 'exist', if not in and through time? A timeless God would be even more different from the things we usually speak about, which are located in our familiar world of space and time.

However we resolve this particular theological question, we may agree that our human words are mostly going to be inadequate when we apply them to God. What to do, then? How should we speak of this different ('other') God?

TO DO

Explore the ways in which how we talk about God should be different from talking about everyday objects or people.

I describe below the main ways in which Christians have responded to the problem of talking about God.

Silence

This is the most extreme option. If there really is an *infinite* difference between God and the (human) world, then 'no concepts which are applicable to the world of experience can be truthfully applied to God' (Brümmer, 1992, p. 41). If God is *so* different from human beings, we must recognize that language about ourselves is wholly inadequate for describing God. As Vincent Brümmer puts it, there could be 'no similarity in meaning at all between the word "love" with reference to God and the word "love" with reference to people'. If this is the case, then silence has to be the preferred theological currency.

There is a certain consistency in this view, and it appears to have been adopted by those mystics, in many religious traditions, who have claimed not only that their mystical experience is beyond words, but also that God, too, is beyond all description. Christian proponents of such views are sometimes said to be following a 'negative way' (*via negativa*) by endorsing only denials within their theology. God is not this or that, they say – God is not, indeed, *any* of the things God is called. God truly 'transcends' ('surpasses', 'goes beyond the limits of') *all* such descriptions. On this view, we cannot really apply any human language to the transcendent God. (This is sometimes described as 'apophatic' theology and is significant within Eastern Orthodoxy.)

But even a denial says something. To say that God is not x gives a sort of account, if a very broad and negative one, of the nature of God. Or does it? Pseudo-Dionysius the Areopagite, a fifth-century Syrian mystic, wrote that the 'true initiate' is plunged

unto the Darkness of Unknowing wherein he renounces all the apprehensions of his understanding and is encouraged in that which is wholly intangible and invisible ... and being united by his highest faculty to Him that is wholly Unknowable, of whom thus by a rejection of all knowledge he possesses a knowledge that exceeds his understanding ... Ascending yet higher we maintain that It is not soul, or mind ... nor can the reason attain to It to name It or to know It. (in Stace, 1960, pp. 136–7)

Perhaps silence is the only proper, if the most extreme, response to the problem of speaking about such a God, such an 'It'. The more strongly we are convinced of the 'mysterious, infinite, and transcendent character of God', the more likely we are to treat any words about this God as being 'so inadequate to be worthless – or even blasphemous' (Wiles, 1976, p. 58).

However, other approaches tread the more 'positive way' of attempting to describe God using human language, providing different types of 'affirmative theology'.

Analogies

When we use an analogy we are claiming that there is some sort of *likeness* between the thing that the word we are using is normally applied to – and therefore what is usually meant by it – and what we are trying to describe. But as a rule we recognize that in employing the word in this way we are stretching its meaning when compared with what it usually means. So this likeness is really a likeness-with-difference.

We do this all the time, even outside theology. So we say that a certain climate is 'healthy', meaning that it tends to help people become and remain healthy; for the word normally applies to people not things. Or we describe our domestic pets as 'intelligent', without implying that they would score anywhere near 100 on a standard (human) IQ test. Or we apply the verb 'living' to such different things as cows and cauliflowers (at least before they arrive on our plates), and corals, chrysalids and coffee beans (at least before we roast them). We even talk of electrical circuits or TV broadcasts as being 'live'. Our language is quite stretchable.

Can we stretch it so far that it embraces God as well? Well, we do this when we claim that God 'lives', 'loves' or 'acts', and even when we say God 'exists'. God clearly does not have the sort of life that biological organisms have – a life that involves nutrition, respiration, reproduction, and so on; nor can God experience or act quite as we do now, as God has no body like ours. (Think how you could perceive or act in the world if you existed only as a disembodied mind without hands or eyes.) Further, the existence of God is unlike existence in our dimensions of space and time. Nevertheless, with some stretching, these words may be applied. God's love, care, thoughts are *like* ours; but also unlike them in many ways.

'Thomists', who are influenced by the writings of Thomas Aquinas (see Chapter 8), sometimes put it this way:

God lives/loves/exists in a way appropriate to God's nature (in God's own way);
just as we live/love/exist in our own way.

Similarly, you might say that your cat is 'intelligent', but in a way that is appropriate to being a cat, 'in a cat's own way', which is analogous to – but not identical with – human forms of intelligence.

Thomists claim that analogy is a *literal* use of language, in which words are used 'in their proper sense', as Aquinas put it. They propose the following test to show this. Does God *really* (in this sense, 'literally') live, love and act; indeed, does he *really* 'exist'? If the answer is 'yes', then we are using these words in a literal sense, even if it is with an analogical (stretched) meaning.

Metaphors

When we apply language to God *figuratively*, however, it fails this test. Is God *really* a rock; has he really got a 'strong arm'? Well no, not literally. God isn't made of stone; God doesn't have any biceps. Being made of solid mineral matter or having muscles (however well developed) is not truly compatible with God's nature. Nevertheless, we do apply these words (or 'images' or 'symbols') to God; but we do so in a figurative, rather than a literal manner.

As is the case with analogies, *metaphors* are very common in our everyday language. There just aren't enough words in the dictionary to describe literally all the things that exist even within this world. So we borrow words that literally apply to something else – carrying them across from one application to the other, and so illuminating and giving descriptive insight to this other thing. Your daughter or sister may be said to have a 'dewy' complexion or a 'fiery' tempera-ment, or to possess a 'slippery' manner (and a 'silver tongue'?) in response to your direct questions. Perhaps she was a bit 'wooden' as well, in her part in the last local amateur dramatic production. You don't mean any of these things literally; but there is a sense in which you truly do mean what you say by them – you mean them seriously. Literal talk is not the only sort of serious talk we engage in, not by a long chalk. (Which is another metaphor, of course. Where did *that* one come from?)

The same goes for much of our language about God. The nouns, adjectives, adverbs and verbs of theological speech are often drawn from language about human beings – or even from Nature more widely – and are then carried across to apply to God, so that we see the one thing (God) in terms of another, very different, thing. So we use language about rocks, shields, fortresses, muscular arms and so on, and apply this language metaphorically to God. (And we do the same thing, most people would argue, when we talk of God using language about shepherds and fathers as well.)

We are well advised to avoid the temptation of taking meta-phors literally in our ordinary language, so as to prevent the sort of confusion (or quarrel) that results from responding too literally in conversation: 'Come, come, my dear, how can I possibly be a "pig" – where's the curly tail?', or 'it is because we have no bread' (Mark 8.14–16; cf. John 6.35). We should resist even more strenuously the inclination to take such language literally when it is applied to God, who is our fortress yet is alive and caring – and so, *in these ways*, is not at all like a building made of wood, brick or stone.

We needn't worry too much about the differences between

analogies and metaphors. After all, metaphors need an element of similarity – a core of analogy – within them in order to work. (Some scholars see the differences between analogy and metaphor as only a difference of degree, and may place 'father' in either category.) But we *do* need to be able to spot the extent to which religious language serves as a *good* analogy or metaphor for God and God's activity, and the ways in which it doesn't succeed in this task – and can therefore mislead us.

TO DO

Try to distinguish the positive element in each of these terms (what it has in common with God) from the negative content (the features it does not share). I offer two worked examples first, which you might be able to extend.

God is ...	✓ *positive elements*	✗ *negative elements*
'alive'	active agent	no reproduction
	aware of others	no body
	....	....
'father'	caring, sustaining, origin	not male
	....	....
'potter'		
'lion'		
'mother'		
'teacher'		
'king'		
'husband'		
'judge'		
'light'		

You could also use a Bible concordance,[1] or the Internet, to find where these terms are applied to God in the Bible, and in what context.

---

1 A concordance provides an alphabetical list of all the words in a text, indicating the passages that contain them.

Myths and parables

These days the word 'myth' is normally understood as an untruth or even a deliberate falsehood. In light of this, new students of theology may be forgiven for rather bridling at the suggestion that the Bible contains any myths. But in the study of religion, a myth is a neutral term for a text that has two features:

- it is a narrative about the relationships between the divine and human realms, in which God or the gods interact in a visible and physical way with human beings;
- it has a great influence on religious believers, and expresses their deepest values and the inner meaning of their faith.

One scholar, Ninian Smart, coined a phrase that nicely brings together the narrative (story) and the affective (passionate) aspects of a myth, calling it 'a moving picture of the sacred'. Analogies and metaphors are often used to paint a portrait or 'still picture' of the deity: as compassionate shepherd, strong rock or loving father. But the myth provides a 'movie', a moving picture – with God 'coming down at Christmas' or 'sending his Spirit as a dove', and the risen, ascended Son of Man 'seated at the right hand' of God or 'coming with the clouds of heaven' (Mark 14.62).

If God may truly be said to do these things, even if our account of them is only a metaphorical one, then these myths or 'story-metaphors' are *true* myths. They correspond (or will correspond) with reality, although this includes the transcendent reality of heaven and God, as well as the physical reality of earth and human beings. It is a true story, even if it is not literally true, for God does not literally 'come down' from anywhere in the third dimension of our space. (God is not literally 'up there' or even 'in my heart'.) We may say that such mythic language is true, although it certainly isn't literally true.

Parables take this one step further. A lot of novels and poems work like myths, as do many traditional fables and legends. They express deep truths, often of a moral nature, about human beings and their relationships; but 'literally' (historically) they are false. Jesus' parables are fictional stories that tell profound, theological truths about our relationship with God. Yes, they are *fictions*: Jesus was not talking about a real good Samaritan or prodigal son, but telling a story to make a point about the reality of God and God's relationship with – not one, but many – real human beings. He spoke true fiction.

Some scholars interpret whole books in the Old Testament – such as Ruth, Jonah and even Job – in the same way, as theological novellas. Does this matter? If we insist that only historical events can speak of God, we shall find ourselves using a rather smaller Bible than the one we have been given, and our Scriptures will be diminished rather than strengthened in their authority, religious value and power. (This is not to say that the book of Jonah *is* a 'made-up' story, only that it doesn't really matter if it were. It can still be true in this deeper, theological sense.)

Jesus' parables are essentially *similes*, and a simile is an explicit metaphor. Instead of saying, 'Jeff Astley *is* a pig' (a metaphor), people might say 'Jeff Astley is *like* a pig' (a simile). Many of the parables begin with the formula, 'The Kingdom of God[2] is like ...' (cf. Luke 13.18):

- yeast (Matthew 13.33);
- treasure in a field, a merchant finding a valuable pearl, a net cast into the sea (Matthew 13.44–50);
- a mustard seed (Mark 4.30–32; cf. Luke 13.19), and so on.

Other comparisons with God are drawn without the use of this formula, for example as:

- a sower (Mark 4.3–8);
- the owner of a vineyard (Mark 12.1–11);
- the father of the 'prodigal son' (Luke 15.11–32);
- a woman who lost a coin (Luke 15.8–10);

---

2 'Kingdom of heaven' in Matthew – which is only a more roundabout way of speaking of God.

- a king who invited guests to a feast (Matthew 22.1–10), and so on.

God or God's Kingdom is not literally a mustard seed, a farmer or whatever, not in every respect; but there is still an illuminating likeness here. These stories *do* reveal something of what the character and activity of God is like. The story narrates who God is as well as what he does, just as novels and anecdotes tell us truths about the nature of human beings. But God is not a human person, and we are forced to tell these sort of stories about God's character and activity because no film or video could ever record the doings of God, as they might have done if God had really been a sower. Stories allow us to portray that which cannot literally be portrayed but is still real, in a likeness that incorporates inevitable differences.

Plain speaking about God

But can we never be literal about God, applying descriptions to God that mean exactly what they mean when we use them about human beings – without even the stretching of meaning of an analogy?

Some have attempted this, and failed. In Mormonism the Godhead contains physically separated beings, with both the Father (Elohim) and the Son having perfect material bodies. Such views, however, end up with an 'anthropomorphic' God – that is, a God who is pictured 'in the form of a man'. Similar approaches would lead to God being perceived *literally* as a Big-Daddy-in-the-(literal) sky, perhaps with a white beard, and stretching out a (presumably muscular) literal right arm (see Job 40.9; Psalm 44.1–3; 89.8–13; cf. Revelation 1.12–16). But even when medieval and later artists illustrated God in this way, on their canvasses and the walls and ceilings of churches, they were painting *symbols*. Symbols are things that 'stand for' something else, and these pictures of a human God obviously stand for a transcendent, infinite God that cannot really be portrayed.

> ## TO DO
>
> Collect together as many concrete, anthropomorphic images of God as you can, from sources such as stained glass in local churches, and sculptures, paintings or illuminated books in museums and art galleries. (The Internet is a good source of such things.)
>
> List their positive and negative elements as representations of God.

However, we *can* sometimes use literal language of God. Some technical theological terms have been so specified that they apply *only* to God, and cannot be applied to human beings. We may take such technical terms literally, and we do this when we affirm that God is (literally) 'uncreated', 'eternal', 'incorporeal' (without a body) – and perhaps, too, when we confess God as 'triune' (Three-in-One), at least in a technical sense. But note that many of these are negative descriptions, portraying God as *not* created, *not* in time, etc. You will recall that this tells us something about God, but not much.

Some philosophers of religion argue that many human terms have an abstract core meaning in terms of *function* that can be applied literally to God. So while 'what it is for God to make something' is very different from what it means for us to do so, there is still 'an abstract feature in common ... that by the exercise of agency something comes about' (Alston, 1987, p. 24).

Mystery and models

Theologians and writers in other subjects (e.g. the philosophy of science) often refer to another type of language: linguistic *models*. These are not to be confused with physical models, which frequently serve as three-dimensional representations of a larger thing – as in the case of model villages, or those detailed models of cars or planes that some people make or collect. A linguistic model does not directly 'picture' the thing it refers to; it depicts it in a less straight-forward and more partial, tentative and figurative way.

Models develop out of metaphors, and are best understood as more conceptualized, and thus more stable and more useful meta-phors, occupying a 'further step along the route from metaphorical to conceptual language' (McFague, 1983, p. 23). But they are not as abstract, clear or unambiguous as a concept.

Nevertheless, models in theology are *developed* metaphors, designed so that they are more accurate, qualified and specific. This enables us to draw some clearer implications from them – just as scientists do, when they 'model' light as waves, like those that travel across water (and sometimes as particles, thought of as inter-acting like billiard balls). Models can be used more systematically than metaphors or images, and frequently turn up in theological argument.

TO DO

Pick out the metaphorical models in these biblical texts and suggest what they imply about the nature of God, Christ, salvation, the Church or heaven: Psalm 23 and 47; Hosea 11.1–4, 8–9; John 1.1–5; 15.1–10; 1 Corinthians 12.12–31; Ephesians 2.13–22; Hebrews 1.1–4; Revelation 21.1–2, 22–25.

The careful use of models that have more precise meanings than the metaphors on which they are based allows us to draw out further implications from our talk of God, Christ and the Church (e.g. God as ruler or judge; Christ as Word, and his death as a victory or sacrifice; the Church as a body). As we saw above (pp. 73, 75), *specifying* our analogous or metaphorical God-talk, by distinguishing its positive and negative components, gives us the same advantage: it allows us to say what follows from it, what it implies. Unless goodness and wisdom in God is something like what it is in human beings, we can have no idea what is implied by saying that God is 'good' or 'wise'. How can we reason in theology (see Chapters 2 and 3) unless we can specify to some extent what we mean by our God-talk? The risk of not doing this is that we end up not being able to draw any conclusions from the language we use about God.

We may confess that God is 'king', but the real theological question is: what does that *mean*? If God is judge, can he show mercy? If Christ's death is a victory, is the war at an end?

Perhaps the greatest danger, however, is to swing too far in the opposite direction, by specifying our analogies too much, and especially by misreading metaphors and models as literal descriptions – rather than as 'partial and inadequate ways of imaging what is not observable' (Barbour, 1974, p. 48). God must always, in the end, be a *mystery*: anything less would not be God. Theological language is therefore never more than an attempt to be articulate about a mystery: it 'will never give us a blueprint of God'. Theologians are forced to talk of God in models and metaphors 'in order to understand, as best they can, a mystery' that is bound to exceed their language (Ramsey, 1957, pp. 164, 171).

This task is continuous with Scripture. Thus the majestic and beautiful Hebrew poetry of Isaiah 40 uses a great deal of descriptive language about God in order to give us an impressive sense of God's character, scope and power; while at the same time affirming that God is unlike all his 'likenesses' – incomparable, unequalled, other and transcendent.

TO DO

Read Isaiah 40. How effective is it as theology?

In doing theology we are pushing the limits of the mystery of God, while trying to safeguard that mystery. If we push too hard in one direction, our idea of God will turn into some (merely) superhuman figure. But if we give up too soon, our theology will quickly come to an end, in our refusal to say anything specific about God. Everything will then be not only mystery, but also silence. This is the theologian's difficult – but essential – balancing act.

There are two respected ways in which theology has justified its use of human language about God:

- Some begin with the claim that God has created the universe and, within it, human beings in his own 'image' and 'likeness' (Genesis 1.26–27; and 'as male and female', despite my use of a masculine pronoun for God). If this is the case, we may think of some 'analogy of being' between creator and creation. In particular, as God causes *us* to be 'good' and 'wise' (within human limits) then God must be truly good and wise (without limits).

- For others, this smacks too much of reading God's attributes off the world. But the world is not God, because it is always creature not creator, and/or because it has fallen away from its original perfection. We should look, then, to God's revelation and salvation, rather than God's original act of creation. This view rejects any 'divine likeness of the creature even in the fallen world' (Barth, 1975, p. 41), and forces us to see true theology as *God's word about Godself*. Only God is truly 'father', and it is God's revelation that shows us this and teaches us that we may talk of God using this word. (Human fathers are poor imitations.) So God, rather than Nature, shows us what God is like.

Which position do you prefer? Either one allows us to keep our nerve in applying the same terms to both God and human beings. And that, at least, keeps theology going.

Further reading

Astley, J., 2004, *Exploring God-Talk*, London: Darton, Longman & Todd.

Astley, J., 2010, *SCM Studyguide to Christian Doctrine*, London: SCM Press, Ch. 3.

Avis, P., 1999, *God and the Creative Imagination: Metaphor, Symbol and Myth in Religion and Theology*, London: Routledge.

Fawcett, T., 1974, *The Symbolic Language of Religion: An Introductory Study*, London: SCM Press.

Macquarrie, J., 1994, *God-Talk: An Examination of the Language and Logic of Theology*, London: SCM Press.

McFague, S., 1982, *Metaphorical Theology: Models of God in Religious Language*, London: SCM Press.

McGrath, A. E., 2007, *Christian Theology: An Introduction*, Oxford: Blackwell, pp. 193–200.

Stiver, D. R., 1996, *The Philosophy of Religious Language: Sign, Symbol and Story*, Oxford: Blackwell, Chs 2 and 6.

8

Modelling Theology:
Classic and Contemporary Examples

When Christian theology is taught in a university setting, it some-times takes the form of a study of the history of theology, or – even in wholly secular settings – an exercise in 'historical theology' (see Chapter 6). Many years ago, theologians who had learned their theology in other places often quipped that those who studied at Oxford University were well grounded in theology, but only up to the middle of the fifth century AD.[1] Admittedly, this was a key date in the historical development of Christian doctrine, but theology didn't stop then. (The syllabus at Oxford is very different now.)

In fact there were a number of periods of significant theological discussion, debate and development. It will be useful to sweep over them here, swooping down occasionally to listen to what a very few Christian thinkers were saying in different periods. The 2,000-year timespan of Christian theology may be divided up into five periods:

- the New Testament period (mainly c. 50–100);
- the patristic period (especially c. 100–451);
- the Middle Ages (c. 700–1500);
- the Reformation (mainly in the sixteenth century);
- the Modern Age (the eighteenth century to the present day).

We must not fall into the trap, however, of thinking that writers from a particular period all thought the same way. The passages below

---

1 *Anno Domini*, 'in the year of our Lord', increasingly now designated CE (for 'Common Era').

sometimes reveal the different concerns, arguments and beliefs of theologians who were writing at the same time.

New Testament times

This is the period in which the books of the New Testament were written: from the date of Paul's first letter to the Christians at Thessalonica (still argued about, but around AD 50) to what is perhaps the last of the New Testament books, 2 Peter (if that is dated between 125 and 140). It is often called the 'apostolic age' because of its link with Jesus' apostles, a group who were of increasing interest and increasingly revered in subsequent centuries.

It may seem odd to some to include these years in a survey of Christian theology, if theology is thought of as the later theological thinking that built on (and developed from?) a biblical foundation. Others prefer to treat it as the *only* authentic period of Christian theology. Certainly, it is a period of unique authority, and shows a distinctiveness, vigour and originality that can only rarely be matched by later periods. This is the great – for some, the exclusive – period of written Christian revelation, representing God's self-disclosure in Jesus, in and through the writings of the friends of Jesus and the authentic witnesses of this revelation, and the texts that came from those who carried forward his gospel and missionary message. (The words 'apostle' and 'mission' derive respectively from the Greek and Latin verbs for 'to send'.)

It is true that much of the material in the New Testament is better described as religion rather than theology, including as it does religious confession, blessings, hymns, prayers, exhortation, guidance, etc., as well as reports of religious experiences and responses to religious events. But these texts also contain much reflective discourse about God, particularly in the distinctive theological voices of Paul and of Jesus himself, as well as of the 'Evangelists' (the authors of the four Gospels) and various writers of letters (or 'epistles') to the early Church communities. So the work of biblical scholars routinely includes the uncovering, clarification, analysis – and, sometimes, theological reflection on – 'the theology/theologies of the New Testament'.

TO DO

Choose a favourite or a controversial passage from a New Testament letter, by Paul or another author. How would you characterize its style, concerns and likely context?

In what ways does its theology address or challenge your beliefs?

What questions would you like to be able to put to its author?

Patristic period

The word 'patristic' (and 'patristics' – the name applied to the study of this period) originates in the Greek for the 'Fathers' of the Church: that is, its early leaders (mostly bishops) and theological scholars. These include early figures such as Ignatius, Justin Martyr and Tertullian, the second-century Irenaeus and Clement (of Alexandria) and the third-century Cyprian. The theology of Athanasius was particularly influential at the first of the Church's great 'ecumenical Councils' at Nicaea in 325, which declared that Christ – the Son or Word – was one in being with God the Father. The theology of Cyril of Alexandria and Pope Leo I similarly influenced the major Council of Chalcedon in 451, which defined Christ as one person with two natures – as both truly divine and truly human.

Many of these early Christian theologians spoke and wrote Greek, and drew on a rich tradition of Greek philosophy that had originated in the work of Plato and Aristotle. (A brief passage from Gregory of Nazianzus appears below.) These 'Greek Fathers' were situated in the eastern ('Byzantine') part of the Roman Empire, in locations such as Antioch, Alexandria, Cappadocia and Constantinople, and their work still dominates the Eastern Orthodox Churches. These regions were conquered in the seventh century by the followers of Islam, however, and eastern Christianity tended to be preoccupied from that time by survival more than theological innovation (Pelikan, 1974, pp. 227–42).

The 'Latin Fathers', for example the great Augustine of Hippo, belonged to the Latin-speaking churches in North Africa and the western parts of the Empire that we now think of as Europe, including its capital, Rome. The Latin Fathers often drew on a more practical and less speculative form of philosophy, and were influenced by legal thinking. Their theologies, especially that of Augustine, came to dominate the 'Western Church' and its later branches of Roman Catholicism and Protestantism.

Gregory of Nazianzus (330–89)

If anyone has put his trust in him as a man without a human mind, he is himself devoid of mind and unworthy of salvation. For what he [Christ] has not assumed he has not healed; it is what is united to his Deity that is saved ... Let them not grudge us our entire salvation, or endue the saviour only with the bones and nerves and appearance of humanity. ('An Examination of Apollinarianism', from Bettenson, 1967, p. 45)

Augustine (354–430)

God created man [humanity] aright, for God is the author of natures, though he is certainly not responsible for their defects. But man was willingly perverted and justly condemned, and so begot perverted and condemned offspring. For we were all in that one man, seeing that we all *were* that one man who fell into sin through the woman who was made from him before the first sin. (Augustine, *City of God*, book xiii, ch. 14)

Middle Ages

The 'medieval'[2] period marks the period between the patristic period and the *renaissance* of the fourteenth to the sixteenth centuries – the 'renascence' or revival of interest in 'classical' (that is, ancient Greek and Latin) philosophy and other literature. Renaissance authors tended to dismiss this intervening period, but it is now recognized as producing much significant theology, particularly theology concerned with issues such as the relationship of reason to faith, and the theology of the Church and the sacraments.

For the historical reason already mentioned, these were largely developments within western theology in the still undivided 'Catholic' (meaning 'universal') Church. Great names of the period include the Scottish theologian Duns Scotus, the English theologian William of Ockham and the Italian Dominican friar Thomas Aquinas, who became very influential indeed in later centuries. These scholars were associated with the new 'schools' or medieval universities such as Paris and Oxford, and are therefore sometimes called 'schoolmen' or 'scholastics'. The latter term also marks their commitment to understanding Christian beliefs by the rigorous application of philosophy, and their willingness to engage in theological speculation that drew equally on Scripture, tradition and philosophy.

The eleventh-century writer Anselm (an Italian who became Archbishop of Canterbury) became a significant figure in Christian theology through his framing of what has become known as the 'ontological argument' for the existence of God (claiming that God must necessarily exist), as well as his attempt to deduce a theory of the atonement (the reconciliation between God and humanity) in his text, *Cur Deus Homo?* ('Why [did] God [become] Man?').

Anselm (1033–1109)

Let us consider whether God could properly remit sin by mercy alone without satisfaction. So to remit sin would be simply to

---

2 A nineteenth-century term, from the Latin for 'middle age'.

abstain from punishing it. And since the only possible way of correcting sin, for which no satisfaction has been made, is to punish it; not to punish it, is to remit it uncorrected. But God cannot properly leave anything uncorrected in His kingdom. Moreover, so to remit sin unpunished, would be treating the sinful and the sinless alike, which would be incongruous to God's nature. And incongruity is injustice.

It is necessary, therefore, that either the honour taken away should be repaid, or punishment should be inflicted. Otherwise one of two things follows – either God is not just to Himself, or He is powerless to do what He ought to do. A blasphemous supposition. (*Cur Deus Homo?*, from Bettenson, 1967, p. 138)

Thomas Aquinas (1225–74)

The body of Christ can only come to be in the sacrament by means of the conversion of the substance of bread into his body; and that which is converted into anything does not remain after the conversion … This conversion is not like natural conversions but is wholly supernatural, brought about only by the power of God … It is obvious to our senses that after consecration all the accidents [something that exists in another thing] of bread and wine remain. And, by divine providence, there is a good reason for this. First, because it is not normal for people to eat human flesh and to drink human blood; in fact, they are revolted by this idea. Therefore Christ's flesh and blood are set before us to be taken under the appearances of those things which are of frequent use, namely bread and wine. Secondly, if we ate our Lord under his proper appearance, this sacrament would be ridiculed by unbelievers. Thirdly, in order that, while we take the Lord's body and blood invisibly, this fact may avail towards the merit of faith. (Aquinas, *Summa Theologiae*, IIIa, question 75)

Reformation

The Protestant Reformation is particularly associated with the names of Martin Luther and the more systematic theologian, John Calvin. They influenced two great streams of Church renewal: the Lutheran Churches, mainly in Germany and Scandinavia, and the Calvinist (sometimes called 'Presbyterian' or 'Reformed') Churches, originating in Switzerland but rapidly influencing Christians in Germany, France, Scotland and England. Both streams of Protestant Christianity are now widely represented in the USA and in Christian communities worldwide that originated through missions.

The intention of these classical reformers was a re-formation of the Church and the removal of what were seen as abuses in the Church's practice and doctrine. Much stress was placed on doctrines such as: justification (being placed in the right relationship to God) by grace through faith alone, without any reliance on human works; the continuing deleterious effects of the 'fall of man' on human freedom and reason; the insistence that Scripture alone contained what was essential for salvation; and ideas of ministry and Church that were thought to have been held in the earliest years of Christianity.

The Catholic (now properly called 'Roman Catholic') Church went through its own reformation – the Catholic or 'Counter' Reformation – during this period, with its theological position being defined over against Protestantism at the Council of Trent (1544–63).

Martin Luther (1483–1546)

A good or a bad house does not make a good or a bad builder; but a good or a bad builder makes a good or a bad house. And in general, the work never makes the workman like itself, but the workman makes the work like himself. So it is with the works of man. As the man is, whether believer or unbeliever, so also is his work – good if it was done in faith, wicked if it was done in unbelief. But the converse is not true, that the work makes the man either a believer or an unbeliever. As works do not make a man a believer, so also they do not make him righteous. But as faith makes a man a believer and righteous, so faith does good works. Since, then, works justify no one, and a man must be right-eous before he does a good work, it is very evident that it is faith alone which, because of the pure mercy of God through Christ and in his Word, worthily and sufficiently justifies and saves the person. A Christian has no need of any work or law in order to be saved since through faith he is free from every law and does everything out of pure liberty and freely. He seeks neither benefit nor salvation since he already abounds in all things and is saved through the grace of God because in his faith he now seeks only to please God. (*The Freedom of a Christian*, from Dillenberger, 1961, p. 70)

John Calvin (1509–64)

When we attribute foreknowledge to God we mean that all things have ever been, and eternally remain, before his eyes; so that to his knowledge nothing is future or past, but all things are present; and present not in the sense that they are reproduced in imagin-ation (as we are aware of past events which are retained in our memory), but present in the sense that he really sees and observes them placed, as it were, before his eyes. And this foreknowledge extends over the whole universe and over every creature. By pre-destination we mean the eternal decree of God, by which he has decided in his own mind what he wishes to happen in the case of each individual. For all men are not created on an equal foot-ing, but for some eternal life is pre-ordained, for others eternal damnation. (*Institutes of the Christian Religion*, book III, ch. xxi, 5, from Bettenson, 1967, p. 214)

TO DO

Review all the extracts above from patristic, medieval and Reformation theologians.

Has anything especially struck you about any of these passages, with regard to its style, concerns, arguments or beliefs?

Which passages best transcend their context and speak in a relevant way to *you*? Can you say why some other passages do not 'work' in the same way?

The Modern Age

Naturally enough, everyone has thought that they lived in this age, because 'modern' simply means 'of the present or recent times' (from the Latin *modo*, 'just now'). *Our* modern age began a while back, with the rise of the empirical sciences, notably dominated by physicists such as Isaac Newton (1642–1727), and of 'modern philosophy', which began with René Descartes' reconstruction of philosophy in a quest for certainty based not on the authority of the Bible or classical authors, but on systematic doubt about all prior assumptions. Such influences led to a great eighteenth-century 'Enlightenment' or 'Age of Reason' that dominated philosophy and theology, responding to Immanuel Kant's injunction to 'dare to use your own reason'. This emphasis on reason was soon challenged, however, by a Romanticism that reasserted passion and imagination, and a concern for experience and feeling in theology – as with the German theologian Friedrich Schleiermacher and the (earlier) English Methodist revival under John Wesley.

Many theological developments followed, ranging from very rational defences of religious belief to challenges to reason from the Christian existentialists, and the rejection of liberal theology and assertion of the pre-eminence of biblical revelation in the work of the Swiss Calvinist theologian Karl Barth and his many followers.

In the twentieth century, theology took a wide variety of forms, with a polarization between conservative and liberal (even radical) accounts of Christian theology in both Protestant and Catholic traditions.

Currently, theology is variously influenced by such diverse streams and influences as:

- the liberal Catholic views that dominated the Second Vatican Council in the 1960s;
- liberation theologies of Latin America and elsewhere, focusing on the liberation of the poor from injustice and economic oppression;
- feminist theology, with its criticism of the silencing of women in the Church and of other masculine biases in Christian theology;
- 'postmodern' approaches that reject the idea of any one dominating philosophical or theological 'story' (cf. pp. 63, 106) that is structured by Enlightenment criteria of reason, clarity and certainty. Postmodernism dismisses both atheistic and religious forms of modern (or 'modernist') thought, endorsing instead the validity of many different, limited, uncertain and particular perspectives – no one of which is viewed as an absolute authority or truth;
- postmodern Christian theologians who express a new respect for the theology of their predecessors, not least Aquinas and Augustine, and embrace a revival of traditional doctrine (e.g. in British 'radical orthodoxy');
- a more general (and largely American) 'postliberal' understanding of Christian theology 'as an act of communal self-description' (Franke, 2005, p. 30), influenced by the work of George Lindbeck;
- theologies that take seriously Christianity's relation to particular influential strands of contemporary thought, including the natural sciences (e.g. 'process theology', which developed a philosophical understanding of God as dynamic and relational, rather than an unmoved being), the social sciences, aspects of culture and other religious traditions;

- conservative Protestant theologians who continue to emphasize classical Reformation doctrines and even fundamentalist views on Scripture; and Roman Catholic theologians who adopt more traditional, pre-Vatican II claims on topics such as the teaching authority of the Church in matters of faith and morals.

Karl Barth (1886–1968)

It is not the right human thoughts about God which form the content of the Bible, but the right divine thoughts about men. The Bible tells us not how we should talk with God but what he says to us; not how we find the way to him, but how he has sought and found the way to us; not the right relation in which we must place ourselves to him, but the covenant which he has made with all who are Abraham's spiritual children and which he has sealed once and for all in Jesus Christ. It is this which is within the Bible. The word of God is within the Bible. (Barth, 1928, p. 43)

Hans Küng (b. 1928)

There is no mention in the New Testament of an institutional holiness, of a church which gives as many as possible of its institutions and persons, its places, times and vessels the attribute 'holy'. If the New Testament is concerned with holiness at all, it is concerned with an utterly personal holiness, a basic attitude of 'holiness' for each individual, which means a total orientation on the will of the 'holy God' himself … So the church may be called 'holy' only to the degree that it is called by God himself through Christ in the Spirit as the community of believers and has placed itself at his service, raised above the banality of the world's course by God's liberating concern. (Küng, 1993, p. 141)

George Lindbeck (b. 1923)

Religion cannot be pictured in the cognitivist (and voluntarist) manner as primarily a matter of deliberately choosing to believe or follow explicitly known propositions or directives. Rather, to become religious – no less than to become culturally or linguistically competent – is to interiorize a set of skills by practice and training. One learns how to feel, act, and think in conformity with a religious tradition that is, in its inner structure, far richer and more subtle than can be explicitly articulated. The primary knowledge is not about the religion, nor that the religion teaches such and such, but rather how to be religious in such and such ways. Sometimes explicitly formulated statements of the beliefs or behavioural norms of a religion may be helpful in the learning process, but by no means always. Ritual, prayer, and example are normally much more important. (Lindbeck, 1984, p. 35)

John Hick (1922–2012)

The third possible answer to the question of the relation between salvation/liberation and the cumulative religious traditions can best be called pluralism … If we accept that salvation/liberation is taking place within all the great religious traditions, why not frankly acknowledge that there is a plurality of saving human response to the ultimate divine Reality? Pluralism, then, is the view that the transformation of a human existence from self-centredness to Reality-centredness is taking place in different ways within the contexts of all the great religious traditions. There is not merely one way but a plurality of ways of salvation or liberation. In Christian theological terms, there is a plurality of divine revelations, making possible a plurality of forms of saving human response …

These many different perceptions of the Real, both theistic and non-theistic, can only establish themselves as authentic by their soteriological efficacy [effectiveness in bringing salvation]. The great world traditions have in fact all proved to be realms within which or routes along which people are enabled to advance in the tradition from self-centredness to Reality-centredness. And, since they reveal the Real in such different lights, we must conclude that they are independently valid. (Hick, 1985, pp. 34, 44)

John Meyendorff (1926–92)

Dead traditionalism cannot be truly traditional. It is an essential characteristic of patristic theology that it was able to face the challenges of its own time while remaining consistent with the original apostolic Orthodox faith. Thus simply to *repeat* what the Fathers said is to be unfaithful to their spirit and to the intention embodied in their theology. (Meyendorff, 1978, p. 7)

Phyllis Trible (b. 1932)

Discerning within Scripture a critique of patriarchy, certain feminists concentrate upon discovering and recovering traditions that challenge the culture. This task involves highlighting neglected texts and reinterpreting familiar ones.

Prominent among neglected passages are portrayals of deity as female. A psalmist declares that God is midwife (Psalm 22.9–10): 'Yet thou art the one who took me from my mother's womb; thou didst keep me safe upon my mother's breast.' In turn, God becomes mother, the one upon whom the child is cast from birth: 'Upon thee was I cast from my birth, and since my mother bore me thou hast been my God.' Although this poem stops short of an exact equation, in it female imagery mirrors divine activity. What the psalmist suggests, Deuteronomy 32.18 makes explicit: 'You were unmindful of the Rock that begot you and you forgot the God who gave you birth.'

Though the Revised Standard Version translates accurately 'The God who gave you birth,' the rendering is tame. We need to accent the striking portrayal of God as a woman in labor pains, for the Hebrew verb has exclusively this meaning. (How scandalous, then, is the totally incorrect translation in the Jerusalem Bible, 'You forgot the God who fathered you.') Yet another instance of female imagery is the metaphor of the womb as given in the Hebrew radicals *rhm*. In its singular form the word denotes the physical organ unique to the female. In the plural, it connotes the compassion of both human beings and God. God the merciful (*rahum*) is God the mother. (See, for example, Jeremiah 31.15–22.) Over centuries, however, translators and commentators have ignored such female imagery, with disastrous results for God, man and woman. To reclaim the image of God female is to become aware of the male idolatry that has long infested faith. (Trible, 1982, p. 117)

TO DO

Reflecting on these extracts from theologians of the Modern Age, has anything especially struck you about the style, concerns, arguments or beliefs of any of these passages?

Which passages most directly impact on your own theology, in either a positive or negative way? And what questions would you like to be able to put to their authors?

Further reading

Cunliffe-Jones, H. with Drewery, B., 1978, *A History of Christian Doctrine*, Edinburgh: T. & T. Clark.

Hill, J., 2003, *The History of Christian Thought*, Oxford: Lion.

Lohse, B., 1966, *A Short History of Christian Doctrine*, Philadelphia, PA: Fortress Press.

McGrath, A. E., 2007, *Christian Theology: An Introduction*, Oxford, Blackwell, Part I.

Pelikan, J., 1985, *Jesus through the Centuries: His Place in the History of Culture*, New York: Harper & Row.

Passages from some 250 source texts from the history of Christian theology may be sampled in A. E. McGrath (ed.), *The Christian Theology Reader*, Oxford: Wiley-Blackwell, 2011; and from 62 texts in A. E. McGrath (ed.), *Theology: The Basic Readings*, Oxford: Wiley-Blackwell, 2012.

9

Where to Next?
Theology and the Future

As we saw in Chapter 8, Christian theology has in different ages addressed rather different concerns and emphasized different elements. In this last chapter we should try to anticipate the challenges that theology needs to face today in order to serve the individual and the Church as they think about God in the future. In order to do this, it may help if you reflect on what you have learned from the rest of this book about the nature and practice of Christian theology.

TO DO

Look back through the previous chapters and try to pick out four or five of the key challenges that *you* think that theology will face, in its attempt to speak of God in tomorrow's world.

In addressing the question of the future of theology, I will draw on some of the topics listed by David Ford as 'the most important questions facing theology' in our third millennium (Ford, 2013, pp. 169–76). I will, however, develop some rather different responses to these issues than those that Ford himself suggests.

The question of God

Christianity takes the 'question of God' to be utterly central. Some recent thinkers have sought to retain many of the insights, values and practices of Christianity, and even much of its doctrine, while understanding the term 'God' in a way that is in sharp conflict with traditional Christianity. While such a radical approach often traces its ancestry back to earlier individual theologians and theological traditions – including negative theology and some versions of existentialism – it could be said to have been provoked by the German philosopher Friedrich Nietzsche (1844–1900). Nietzsche told a parable of a madman who proclaims the death of God to the smug atheists in the marketplace, and accuses them (and himself) of God's murder – an act that changes everything, including the foundations of truth and morality. 'Are we not drifting through infinite nothing? … Shall we have to become gods ourselves?'

The 'Death of God' movement of the 1960s recognized the death of God as a cultural phenomenon that theology must address, and even as a theological truth (for Thomas Altizer, God literally died on the cross, emptying himself into the world). The English philosopher of religion Don Cupitt later championed a 'non-realist' religion in which the word 'God' was no more than a potent symbol for certain spiritual and moral ideals: 'God is the role God plays in developing our self-understanding, focussing our aspirations and shaping the course of our lives' (Cupitt, 1986, p. 103).

In contrast to these sympathetic interpretations, increasing numbers of people today espouse an aggressive atheism that condemns or ridicules the traditional notion of a creator and saviour God.

TO DO

How should Christian theology respond to atheist critiques of, or radical Christian reinterpretations of, the concept of God?

Theology, thinking and dialogue

David Ford is particularly interested in the question whether theology can be 'thoughtfully responsible' in its engagement with 'the best thought and research in a multiplicity of rapidly developing fields', and 'adequately hospitable' to such broad pursuits of wisdom (Ford, 2013, pp. 171–2). He is concerned about the suspicion among some Christians of academic education, and of thinking in general.

Do you share this concern? The anti-intellectual stance of many in the Church may lead us to wonder how open they are to truths and insights from other areas of knowledge, let alone from within the variety of types of theological thinking that are pursued within the wider Church. Sometimes Christian criticism of contemporary thought can have the opposite effect from what it intends. While a student of science, I recall hearing several sermons cautioning against the methods and claims of the natural sciences. They merely encouraged me to believe that science and religious belief must be incompatible, which contributed to a period during which I rejected the latter – rather than the former. In some ways, this was by far the easier option. It was only later, when compelled to admit to a deeper response to Christianity within myself, that I felt obliged to take on the struggle of making sense of religious faith in a way that was compatible with my *other* beliefs, especially my scientific beliefs. This was a much harder task, and one for which my former Christian teachers and preachers had not prepared me.

Although Christianity is essentially a religious response, and not a philosophical position, I think that many people are held back from embracing the Christian faith because they suspect that it is not sufficiently intellectually robust or open-minded. You will have noted how often the role of critical reason within theology has been defended in this book. The 'easy yoke' that Jesus offers (Matthew 11.30) should not, I think, be seen as a simple-minded, facile or intellectually *superficial* way. Nevertheless, I repeat, this does not mean that Christianity is essentially a rational exercise or a system of beliefs.

Christianity is both simple and hard. The Christian response and journey are, at base, quite straightforward things. We do not require intellectual sophistication to understand them, nor any superior moral or spiritual stature before we may engage in them. The Christian gospel is not reserved for the clever, the morally squeaky-clean or those who are culturally up-market. Christianity is more ordinary and more everyday than that; and in many ways it is a lot easier than that.

And yet, although it is such an uncomplicated thing to discern and respond to, the call of the gospel is likely to lead us along some very demanding terrain, if we allow it to do so. Much may be demanded of us spiritually and morally; and those who are willing to take it seriously intellectually will find themselves engaged in a lot of strenuous reflection as well. In all these areas it can result in some exhausting hard work and perhaps some wounds along the way, as the first disciples discovered. Nevertheless, for the Christian this journey will always appear as the 'easy way', because for the Christian it is the only way to travel – this easy-hard following of Jesus. (Astley, 2007, pp. ix–x)

TO DO

Having read the various claims in the present book for the importance of reason in the development, critique and justification of Christian belief, how do you now view the place of reason within Christianity in general, and particularly within your own theology?

Another of Ford's questions for the future of theology asks how (using words from his 1999 edition) a 'dialogical and comparative theology' may flourish that takes 'radically different theologies' and faiths – as well as true dialogue between them – *seriously*.

In this book we have discussed how learning theology is always an implicit dialogue or conversation between one's own (initially ordinary) theology and the variety of theologies of the academy and the Church's traditions. Being open to the possibility of changing one's beliefs, in response to the different beliefs of other people, is a matter of being willing enough, and feeling strong enough, to allow ourselves to be faithfully *vulnerable*. This is a fundamental condition of all true learning – a condition of hearing and learning the truth. I would argue that it requires:

- the attitude-virtue of humility (see Chapter 3), as well as an intellectual openness and a confidence that – in the end – all truth is *God's truth*;
- a belief that our truth is, nevertheless, always a *human truth*; and that it is therefore inevitable that it is always going to be inadequate, frail and limited.

Christ is described as being himself the truth, way and life, and not just a route that can eventually lead us to these things (see John 14.6; cf. 8.31–32; 16.12–14; 18.37–38). This personalizes the quest for truth. To learn the truth, any truth, is in some sense and to some extent to have 'learned Christ': to have walked some paces along his Way, in our way, and to have begun to share an aspect of his Life, within our life.

(Even when it doesn't feel like this at all …)

TO DO

Christian theology makes cosmic claims about the significance of Jesus and his truth. In light of this, what should we think about the truth-claims of other religions or 'philosophies of life'?

How should we engage with people of other faiths, and of none, about our beliefs?

Who will do theology?

Ford's answer to this question is: 'those who are gripped by the [theological] questions and who desire to pursue understanding, knowledge, and wisdom by trying to answer them responsibly', while being 'located anywhere in society' (Ford, 2013, p. 175).

The German Protestant theologian Jürgen Moltmann (born 1926), in his personal reflections on a theologian's life, writes both positively and movingly of his view of what I call 'ordinary theology' – and what he calls 'the theology of the people' and the 'common' (or 'general') 'theology of all believers'.

> All Christians *who believe and who think about what they believe* are theologians, whether they are young or old, women or men. That is what Luther meant:
>
> All are theologians, that means every Christian.
>
> All are said to be theologians so that all may be Christians.
>
> ...
>
> Academic theology is nothing other than the scholarly penetration and illumination by mind and spirit of what Christians in the congregations think when they believe in God and live in the fellowship of Christ. (Moltmann, 2000, pp. 11–13)

This gives some priority within theology's future to the great mass of Christians, subordinating even the task of academic theology in order that we take account of what 'ordinary' Christians in the congregations think, and assist its development into a more mature theology.

Does this suggest that the Church's theology ('ecclesiastical theology') should become a more widespread, less clerical or even a more ordinary enterprise? Although theological education inevitably leads to a reformation and modification of our ordinary theology, and often results in its critical correction and pruning, might the future of Christian theology lie in something whose *form* is closer to – and has more of the virtues of – its ordinary theological roots?

TO DO

How important, in your view, are the Church's reserve army of ordinary theologians, billeted weekly in its pews but facing action daily throughout the world, for the Church's future life and thought?

Theology for everyday life

Earlier in his list of questions, Ford makes this comment about the concerns of theology, which he believes should not be confined to matters of religion: 'Theology is obviously concerned too with the shaping of ordinary life in families and relationships, griefs and joys, leisure and work' (Ford, 2013, p. 173). He expects that this fact will lead to a demand for 'theological thoughtfulness' in engaging with a wider range of issues in society, beyond those on which the Church tends to focus. This is theology addressing its third 'audience' (see Chapter 2): not the Church or the academy, but the public sphere – including all of life in general.

In order to engage in this task, theology will need all the resources it can muster. It will need to become a theology for all (and not just clergy) that is also a theology for everyday life. There is an honourable tradition within Christian thinking that emphasizes the importance and sacredness of our ordinary – and, in one sense of that word, 'secular' – life. Both Roman Catholic and Eastern Orthodox traditions have embraced *sacramentality*, which is the view that all reality bears God's presence, actually or potentially, and may thus serve as an instance of God's salvation. This implies a sacramental view of creation that sees this world as a material sign and channel of God's spiritual truth, grace and power. The theology of the Protestant Reformers and later Puritans also sought to return Christian thinking to a focus on the everyday: viewing ordinary life as *the* place for finding God and exercising our religious vocation, instead of limiting these things to the *extra*ordinary locations, disciplines and lifestyles of celibate, 'professional' Christians.

I have argued elsewhere that, as '"ordinary life" itself is the primary locus of our spiritual health', we need 'to take seriously a theology that is grounded in the challenges and fulfilments of ordinary life and its ordinary religious concerns, rather than in the controversies of the academy' (Astley, 2002, pp. 49, 52). Such a theology is a 'theology for all'. It must be a 'theology for the road', for walking the Christian Way. It might even be said to be a theology apt for meeting Christ on *our way* and learning him there, in our homes, streets and workplaces – which are often some distance away from most churchy, monastic or academic settings.

> 'Learning Christ in the ordinary way' is a question of learning the true meaning of Christ, and of learning other things 'in the way of Jesus'; and of doing all this in and from our normal, everyday, workaday, day-by-day life. This 'Christly learning' is also 'godly learning', because to learn Christ on the road is to discover the truth of the gospel and of the Christ-like God. (Astley, 2007, p. 14)

Celebrating variety

I should like to conclude by returning to the theme of the varied, multifaceted nature of Christian belief and understanding. We live in what is often said to be a 'postmodern' age (see p. 93). As we have seen, this means that the culture – and often the philosophy or cast of mind that it encourages – recognizes no one Big Story ('meta-narrative' or 'meganarrative') as the explanation of everything. Instead, with eyes ever open to the screens of our TVs, smartphones and tablets, and transfixed by rolling news and the ever-changing contributions provided by websites, blogs and social media, we (or at least our relatives and neighbours) are immersed in a great variety of competing authorities and voices. It is all rather chaotic – so much diversity! And it is getting worse.

Or better? For there is something to be said for variety, even –

especially – in theology. I believe that Christianity should be taught in all its fullness. This includes not only in its depth, that is to say its 'point', but also in its *breadth* – its 'catholicity' – and therefore its variety. It is inevitable that, when faced by an honest account of the kaleidoscope of Christianity (not least in the area of Christian belief), many of us will feel somewhat dizzy. (Recall what was said about historical theology above, pp. 62–3) After all, as the Roman Catholic theologian Hans Küng once argued, 'everything can be called Christian which in theory and practice has an explicit, positive reference to Jesus Christ' (Küng, 1977, p. 125). And from his rather different, Religious Studies perspective, Ninian Smart exclaimed: 'It is not possible to define an essence of Christianity, beyond saying that the faith relates to Christ, either in historical continuity or through religious experience or both' (Smart, 1979, p. 128).

But isn't this *too* broad a viewpoint?

As we have also seen, serious scholars accept that the Bible contains a wide spectrum of different theologies. The study of Christian theology also involves admitting variety, as does any study of the history of the Church. A plurality of both belief and practice has always existed, across and within the Christian Churches. Is it all too much, all too wide? 'If there is such a thing as Christian unity, it will necessarily be in the form of a containment of diversity within bounds' (Sykes, 1984, p. 240).

Variety with diversity, then; but variety within limits. For not just *anything* can count as being authentically Christian, that's for sure: although different Christians will continue to disagree as to what is, in fact, truly 'of Christ'.

One of the greatest advantages of portraying the variety of Christianity is that it helps to broaden the conversation between our own theology and the teachings (plural) of the Church and the academy. This makes it much more likely that we shall find something in the vast treasure-house of theology to which we can relate, something with which *we* can make a connection. Perhaps that was your experience in reading the passages in Chapter 8?

A willingness to accept variety, difference and plurality is not only necessary for the student of theology. It is essential for any full response to Christianity. Ours is a religion of salvation, and it is intended for everyone. Jesus can only be the Saviour if he is acknowledged by all, and is able to heal all. But if the 'all' is *this* diverse, the salvation – and the Saviour – must be all-embracing, many-sided. The salvation Jesus brought to the woman who had suffered haemorrhages for 12 years (Mark 5.24b–34) was very different from the salvation he brought to the rich tax-collector, Zacchaeus (Luke 19.1–10) – and necessarily so, because their needs, hurts and sins were all different. And if anyone is to say, today or tomorrow, 'You are the Christ, the Son of the Blessed,' it can only be because *their* needs have been met, *their* hurts healed, and *their* sinfulness and misunderstandings not only challenged, but also resolved and redeemed. In *Christ of the Everyday*, I describe this as a proper and wholly acceptable, even inevitable, form of relativism – 'salvific relativism' (Astley, 2007, p. 119).

This is not to say that there isn't in the end one Church, one faith and certainly one Lord. But it is to say that all of these are multifaceted, and therefore multi-dimensional. As another has put it, there is 'one Jesus but many Christs', adding 'I call him Christ insofar as I respond to [his] summons … But the way he is Christ to me may be very different from the way he is Christ for some other person' (Cupitt, 1972, p. 143). This is not only true of Jesus. It is also true of Scripture and tradition – and of Christian worship, ethics and theology as well. There are many ways of being obedient to the Bible and of believing in the creeds. And there are many ways of following Jesus. So Christianity is *internally plural*.

As, of course, is the Church. It is one body, made up of many, very different members: a unity, but never a uniformity.

I want to address my closing words to those who have embarked on a study of theology because they wish to offer themselves for some form of ministry within this varied Church. I believe that the good minister must recognize this variety and be willing to celebrate the Church's 'individual differences' – that is, how the individuals within it differ in their theology and spirituality, as well as in their racial, gender, psychological, social, wealth, class, political, educational and intellectual (and many other) characteristics. In my view, the embracing of variety is essential to all of the Church's pastoral and communicative ministries.

As the popular – and true – cliché has it, 'it wouldn't do if we were all the same'. 'Male and female he created them' is another famous saying (Genesis 1.27) and it is a text that is sometimes treated as a symbol and summary of the almost endless variety of human-kind that God has made 'in his image'. Difference exists within the Church, and only a few will turn out to be clones of their minis-ter, particularly in theology. This is something that you had better get used to. You also need to get used to the variety of Christian theology, and 'get over' the fact that you have to live with a multi-dimensional Christian truth in an increasingly diverse Church.

As we must all do, for we are all in this together.

Theology is manifold. But it remains the truth of the one God, who alone is able to conduct the countless voices of the Church so that they become the Lord's one, universal choir.

TO DO

Our final question, of course, must be: What do *you* think?

Further reading

Astley, J., 2007, *Christ of the Everyday*, London: SPCK, Chs 7 and 8.

Borg, M. J., 2011, *Speaking Christian: Recovering the Lost Meaning of Christian Words*, London: SPCK.

Ford, D. F., 2011, *The Future of Christian Theology*, Oxford: Wiley-Blackwell.

Ford, D. F., 1999, 2013, *Theology: A Very Short Introduction*, Oxford: Oxford University Press, Ch. 10.

Franke, J. R., 2005, *The Character of Theology: An Introduction to its Nature, Task, and Purpose*, Grand Rapids, MI: Baker Academic.

McFague, S., 2008, 'An Epilogue: The Christian Paradigm', in P. Hodgson, and R. King (eds), *Christian Theology: An Introduction to its Traditions and Tasks*, London: SPCK, pp. 377–90.

Migliore, D. L., 2004, *Faith Seeking Understanding: An Introduction to Christian Theology*, Grand Rapids, MI: Eerdmans, Ch. 13 and Appendix C.

You might also dip into some of the essays in Parts III to VIII of D. F. Ford with R. Muers (eds), *The Modern Theologians: An Introduction to Christian Theology since 1918*, Oxford: Blackwell, 2005, for a taste of the variety of modern issues addressed by a range of Christian theologians over the last 100 years.

References

Ackroyd, R. and Major, D., 1999, *Shaping the Tools: Study Skills in Theology*, London: Darton, Longman & Todd.

Alston, W. P., 1987, 'Functionalism and Theological Language', in T. V. Morris (ed.), *The Concept of God*, Oxford: Oxford University Press, pp. 21–40.

Astley, J., 1994, *The Philosophy of Christian Religious Education*, Birmingham, AL: Religious Education Press.

Astley, J. (ed.), 2000, *Learning in the Way: Research and Reflection on Adult Christian Education*, Leominster: Gracewing.

Astley, J., 2002, *Ordinary Theology: Looking, Listening and Learning in Theology*, Aldershot: Ashgate.

Astley, J., 2004, *Exploring God-Talk: Using Language in Religion*, London: Darton, Longman & Todd.

Astley, J., 2007, *Christ of the Everyday*, London: SPCK.

Astley, J., 2010, *SCM Studyguide to Christian Doctrine*, London: SCM Press.

Astley, J. and Day, D. (eds), 1992, *The Contours of Christian Education*, Great Wakering: McCrimmons.

Balthasar, H. U. von, 1960, *Verbum Caro*, I, Einsiedeln: Johannesverlag.

Barbour, I. G., 1974, *Myths, Models and Paradigms: The Nature of Scientific and Theological Language*, London: SCM Press.

Barr, J., 1999, *The Concept of Biblical Theology: An Old Testament Perspective*, London: SCM Press.

Barth, K., 1928, *The Word of God and the Word of Man*, London: Hodder & Stoughton.

Barth, K., 1975, *Church Dogmatics*, I/1, Edinburgh: T. & T. Clark.

Bettenson, H. (ed.), 1967, *Documents of the Christian Church*, Oxford: Oxford University Press.

Boff, C., 2009, *Theology and Praxis: Epistemological Foundations*, Eugene, OR: Wipf & Stock.

Borg, M. J., 2003, *The Heart of Christianity: Rediscovering a Life of Faith*, San Francisco: HarperSanFrancisco.

Bromiley, G. W., 1978, *Historical Theology: An Introduction*, Edinburgh: T. & T. Clark.

Brown, D., 1994, 'Did Revelation Cease?', in A. G. Padgett (ed.), *Reason and the Christian Religion: Essays in Honour of Richard Swinburne*, Oxford: Clarendon Press, pp. 121–41.

Brown, D., 1999, *Tradition and Imagination: Revelation and Change*, Oxford: Oxford University Press.

Brümmer, V., 1992, *Speaking of a Personal God: An Essay in Philosophical Theology*, Cambridge: Cambridge University Press.

Cameron, H. et al., 2010, *Talking about God in Practice: Theological Action Research and Practical Theology*, London: SCM Press.

Clark-King, E., 2004, *Theology by Heart: Women, the Church and God*, Peterborough: Epworth Press.

Cobb, J., 1993, *Becoming a Thinking Christian*, Nashville, TN: Abingdon Press.

Cobb, J., 1994, *Lay Theology*, St Louis, MO: Chalice Press.

Cupitt, D., 1972, 'One Jesus, Many Christs?', in S. W. Sykes and J. P. Clayton (eds), *Christ, Faith and History: Cambridge Studies in Christology*, Cambridge: Cambridge University Press, pp. 131–44.

Cupitt, D., 1986, *Life Lines*, London: SCM Press.

Dillenberger, J. (ed.), 1961, *Martin Luther: Selections from his Writings*, Garden City, NY: Doubleday.

Dunn, J. D. G., 1977, *Unity and Diversity in the New Testament*, London: SCM Press.

Dunn, J. D. G., 2009, *New Testament Theology: An Introduction*, Nashville, TN: Abingdon Press.

Evans, C. F., 1960, 'The Inspiration of the Bible', in L. Hodgson et al., *On the Authority of the Bible: Some Recent Studies*, London: SPCK, pp. 25–32.

Evans, D., 1979, *Struggle and Fulfillment: The Inner Dynamics of Religion and Morality*, Cleveland, OH: Collins.

Ford, D. F., 1999, 2013, *Theology: A Very Short Introduction*, Oxford: Oxford University Press.

Francis, L. J., Robbins, M. and Astley, J., 2005, *Fragmented Faith: Exposing the Fault-Lines in the Church of England*, London: Paternoster Press.

Franke, J. R., 2005, *The Character of Theology: An Introduction to its Nature, Task, and Purpose*, Grand Rapids, MI: Baker Academic.

Graham, E. L., 1996, *Transforming Practice: Pastoral Theology in an Age of Uncertainty*, London: Mowbray.

Green, L., 2009, *Let's Do Theology: Resources for Contextual Theology*, London: Mowbray.

Groome, T. H., 2011, *Will There Be Faith? Depends on Every Christian*, London: Veritas.

Hanson, A. T. and Hanson, R. P. C., 1981, *Reasonable Belief: A Survey of the Christian Faith*, Oxford: Oxford University Press.

Haymes, B., 1988, *The Concept of the Knowledge of God*, London: Macmillan.

Hebblethwaite, B., 1980, *The Problems of Theology*, Cambridge: Cambridge University Press.

Hick, J., 1983, *The Second Christianity*, London: SCM Press.

Hick, J., 1985, *Problems of Religious Pluralism*, London: Macmillan.

Hick, J., 2008, *Who or What is God? And Other Investigations*, London: SCM Press.

Hodgson, P. C., 1994, *Winds of the Spirit: A Constructive Christian Theology*, London: SCM Press.

Hodgson, P. C., 1999, *God's Wisdom: Toward a Theology of Education*, Louisville, KY: Westminster John Knox Press.

Holmer, P. L., 1978, *The Grammar of Faith*, San Francisco: Harper & Row.

Inbody, T., 2005, *The Faith of the Christian Church: An Introduction to Theology*, Grand Rapids, MI: Eerdmans.

Johnson, L. T., 2010, *The Writings of the New Testament: An Interpretation*, London: SCM Press.

Kelsey, D. H., 1992, *To Understand God Truly: What's Theological about a Theological School*, Louisville, KY: Westminster/John Knox Press.

Küng, H., 1977, *On Being a Christian*, London: Collins.

Küng, H., 1993, *Credo: The Apostles' Creed Explained for Today*, London: SCM Press.

Lampe, G. W. H., 1963, 'The Bible Since the Rise of Critical Study', in D. E. Nineham (ed.), *The Church's Use of the Bible: Past and Present*, London: SPCK, pp. 125–44.

Le Guin, Ursula K., 1989, *Dancing at the Edge of the World: Thoughts on Words, Women, Places*, New York: Grove.

Lindbeck, G. A., 1984, *The Nature of Doctrine: Religion and Theology in a Postliberal Age*, London: SPCK.

Macquarrie, J., 1977, *Principles of Christian Theology*, London: SCM Press.

McFague, S., 1983, *Metaphorical Theology: Models of God in Religious Language*, London: SCM Press.

McGrath, A. E., 2007, *Christian Theology: An Introduction*, Oxford: Blackwell.

McGrath, A. E., 2008, *Theology: The Basics*, Oxford: Blackwell.

McIntosh, M. A., 2008, *Divine Teaching: An Introduction to Christian Theology*, Oxford: Blackwell.

Meyendorff, J., 1978, *Living Tradition: Orthodox Witness in the Contemporary World*, Crestwood, NY: St Vladimir's Seminary Press.

Migliore, D. L., 2004, *Faith Seeking Understanding: An Introduction to Christian Theology*, Grand Rapids, MI: Eerdmans.

Moltmann, J., 2000, *Experiences in Theology: Ways and Forms of Christian Theology*, London: SCM Press.

Morgan, R. with Barton, J., 1988, *Biblical Interpretation*, Oxford: Oxford University Press.

Morse, C., 2009, *Not Every Spirit: A Dogmatics of Christian Belief*, New York: Continuum.

Moschella, M. C., 2008, *Ethnography as a Pastoral Practice: An Introduction*, Cleveland, OH: Pilgrim Press.

Pelikan, J., 1974, *The Spirit of Eastern Christendom (600–1700)*, Chicago: University of Chicago Press.

Ramsey, I. T., 1957, *Religious Language: An Empirical Placing of Theological Phrases*, London: SCM Press.

Smart, N., 1979, *The Phenomenon of Christianity*, London: Collins.

Soulen, R. N., 1977, *Handbook of Biblical Criticism*, Guildford and London: Lutterworth Press.

Stace, W. T. (ed.), 1960, *The Teaching of the Mystics*, New York: Mentor Books.

Stiver, D. R., 2009, *Life Together in the Way of Jesus Christ: An Introduction to Christian Theology*, Waco, TX: Baylor University Press.

Swinton, J. and Mowat, H., 2006, *Practical Theology and Qualitative Research*, London: SCM Press.

Sykes, S., 1984, *The Identity of Christianity: Theologians and the Essence of Christianity from Schleiermacher to Barth*, London: SPCK.

Thomas, O. C., 1983, *Introduction to Theology*, Wilton, CT.: Morehouse.

Tilley, T. W., 2000, *Inventing Catholic Tradition*, Maryknoll, NY: Orbis Books.

Tilley, T. W., 2010, *Faith: What It Is and What It Isn't*, Maryknoll, NY: Orbis Books.

Tillich, P., 1957, *Dynamics of Faith*, New York: Harper & Row.

Tillich, P., 1968, *Systematic Theology: Combined Volume*, Vol. One, Welwyn: Nisbet.

Tracy, D., 1981, *The Analogical Imagination: Christian Theology and the Culture of Pluralism*, London: SCM Press.

Trible, P., 1982, 'Feminist Hermeneutics and Biblical Studies', *Christian Century*, 99(4), 3–10 February, pp. 116–18.

Wallis, A., 1981, *The Radical Christian*, Eastbourne: Kingsway.

Weil, S., 1977, *The Simone Weil Reader*, ed. G. A. Panichas, New York: David McKay.

Wiles, M., 1976, *What is Theology?*, Oxford: Oxford University Press.

Williams, R., 2000a, *Lost Icons: Reflections on Cultural Bereavement*, Edinburgh: T. & T. Clark.

Williams, R., 2000b, *On Christian Theology*, Oxford: Blackwell.